THE ART OF BEING ALIVE

SUCCESS THROUGH THOUGHT

BY
ELLA WHEELER WILCOX

HARPER & BROTHERS PUBLISHERS
NEW YORK AND LONDON
MCMXIV

PRINTED IN THE UNITED STATES OF AMERICA
PUBLISHED JULY, 1914
F-O

CONTENTS

CONTENTS

THE ART OF BEING ALIVE

THE ART OF BEING ALIVE

I

ART THOU ALIVE?

Art thou alive? Nay, not too soon reply,
Tho' hand and foot, and lip, and ear, and eye
Respond, and do thy bidding; yet maybe
Grim death has done his direst work with thee.
Life, as God gives it, is a thing apart
From active body and from beating heart.
It is the vital spark, the unseen fire,
That moves the mind to reason and aspire;
It is the force that bids emotion roll,
In mighty billows from the surging soul.

It is the light that grows from hour to hour,
And floods the brain with consciousness of power;
It is the spirit dominating all,
And reaching God with its imperious call,
Until the shining glory of his face
Illuminates each sorrowful, dark place;
It is the truth that sets the bondsman free,
Knowing he will be what he wills to be.
With its unburied dead the earth is sad.
Art thou alive? Proclaim it and be glad.
Perchance the dead may hear thee and arise,
Knowing they live, and HERE is Paradise.

II

BEING ALIVE

Cease wondering why you came—
  Stop looking for faults and flaws;
Rise up to-day in your pride and say,
  "I am part of the First Great Cause!"

IN every thousand people who are living on this earth, not more than one is *alive*.

To be really alive means more than to be a moving, breathing, eating, drinking, and talking human creature.

He who is actually alive finds the days too short for all the wonderful explorations which life offers in three realms to the reverent and aspiring adventurer.

He finds life itself a continual adventure, an unfolding panorama, with opportunities for pleasure and achievement at every turn.

He finds himself an object of interesting study, however dissatisfied he may be with the present results of that study, for he perceives that he is a crude chunk of Eternity, and that in himself lie all the powers and possibilities latent in the

Universe. And that in himself lies the *will* to work out these possibilities.

He who is fully alive enjoys the earth and all its pleasures. He loves the slap of the wind upon his cheek, the dash of the waves upon his breast, the motion of his limbs in the swift walk; the thrill of the good steed's body under his own; the ecstasy of rhythm in the dance; the vibrant swing of the oar. He loves labor, and the fatigue which follows; and in his harmoniously developed frame there is not one lazy or unused muscle.

But being alive does not stop here.

The man who is practising the art of being alive to its full extent has an alert, receptive brain and an awakened spirit. Without these he would simply be a splendid animal. With these he is the highest expression of the Creative Power visible to mortal vision. And with these he finds his opportunities for happiness, usefulness, and pleasure in existence threefold.

He knows the pleasures of the physical plane, for which his body is fashioned; he draws to himself the pleasures of the mental plane, and he senses the pleasures of the spiritual plane, which lies near, and derives power therefrom.

The man who is alive in all these ways must radiate light, cheer, sympathy, and helpfulness to all who come within his aura. Being alive to the vibrations from three realms, he knows all temptations; and from having made many missteps himself, in his road to unfoldment, he can sympathize, counsel, and help onward those who have not been able to keep step with him in his progress.

The man who is really alive realizes that he must use his own position in the world, and his own environment, as the first field of action if he hopes to reach success in any venture. He must not wait for luck or a miracle to give him a change of location and surroundings better suited to his taste. Out of whatever destiny has bestowed upon him he will make the conditions which he desires.

And out of every earth day he will make a little bit of heaven.

No difficulty can discourage, no obstacle dismay, no trouble dishearten the man who has acquired the art of being alive. Difficulties are but dares of fate, obstacles but hurdles to try his skill, troubles but bitter tonics to give him strength; and he rises higher and looms greater after each encounter with adversity.

The man who is wholly alive finds pleasure in the simplest things; and to him nothing is commonplace, nothing is menial. And he is never bored, for nature and human nature and himself are ever interesting subjects of contemplation and study. And the future to him is a radiant vision, growing ever more and more wonderful.

If you are alive you are in touch with every new movement; you are awake to the consciousness of the march of progress and the discoveries of science; and you are lending a listening ear to what the students of metaphysical thought have to say.

If you are dull or indifferent or unbelieving when the great facts relative to this subject are mentioned in your presence, then you are no more alive to the vital truths of the day than is the child unborn, or the victim of the sleeping sickness, who lies for months in a state of lethargy, unable to think or reason, even though not dead. The marvels which exist all about you, the wonderful experiences which are related by thousands of intelligent human beings, who have given time and concentration to the exploration of the mental realm, have appealed to your mind and heart sufficiently to awaken your respectful interest, if you are really *alive.*

If you are bored with life and work, if you think the years of early youth alone are happy years, if you believe sentiment and romance are evanescent feelings, if you find daily life commonplace, if you imagine you are too old or too busy to make something worth while out of your opportunities, then you are not *alive.*

If you believe sickness, poverty, and unhappiness cannot be changed to health, comfort, and peace by yourself, then you are indeed unborn; and if you think elasticity of body and mind, and a joyful outlook, and worthy achievements, and vital joy in life cannot accompany human beings along the way after the half-century mark has been passed, you are not *alive*. You merely exist. And you are losing your wonderful chance to utilize for the good of the world and for your own good, here and hereafter, these golden days by a knowledge and use of the Divine Will in yourself.

Are you alive?

III

THE SCIENCE OF SENSIBLE THINKING

However full the world,
  There is room for an earnest man.
It had need of me, or I would not be—
  I am here to strength the plan.

A FEW years ago the philosophy of "Mind Over Matter" was talked and believed only by advanced thinkers and dreamers, the spiritual-minded and the visionary. Practical, every-day people laughed at or ignored all phases of the new version of a very old science.

It is gratifying and surprising to find how the law is *to-day* being understood and employed in the world.

Not long since a successful manager of two very large hotels was complimented upon the harmony and happiness which pervaded his hotels. Employees and associates all seemed to regard the employer as a personal friend and work as a recreation. The proprietor was a handsome, florid man, of middle age, alert and active. A casual observer would have considered him a man particularly fond of the luxuries of life, and if his ideas of enjoyment had been under discussion one would have said that the race-track and bridge whist took the lead and religious matters were left to the women of his family. Instead, this man, in a conversation regarding his hotel success, remarked that he felt his prosperity was entirely due to the fact that for five years he had been a patient student of *Mental Science*, and was applying its laws to his daily affairs.

"When things go at all wrong with me," he said, "and I feel nervous or out of sorts, I go at once to my room, sit alone, and take a half-hour of concentration, until I grow peaceful. I know I have no right to mix with my employees or guests until I have harmonious conditions within myself. I am my own heaven and hell, my own failure or success. It is not always my fault if things go wrong, but it is my fault if they do not become righted. It is my fault if I do not make a success of whatever I undertake. Until five years ago I had no success in anything. I blamed Fate and conditions and every body and thing but myself. Then I went into the study of Mental Laws and began to learn what a limitless field the mind has and what wonderful powers are contained in the spirit of man, and since then everything has turned my way. Whatever I undertake succeeds, and I have no trouble with help or business associates. Any passing disturbance I can trace to its source and allay."

These words from a practical business man were especially interesting.

The earth has too many expensive churches and too much Sunday religion. What it wants is a religion that is applied every hour of the day in the street and mart and office and home—a religion which helps men to be happy in their work and makes their employees and associates happy. A religion to keep health of body and mind and harmony and hope in the mental atmosphere and to create a heaven right here on earth.

The purpose of this book is to assist those who seek a simple, practical method of applying the laws of Mind to the daily affairs of life.

The book makes no claim of originality of thought or of literary excellence. Its ideas are as old as the universe. The central theme may be found in the Vedas and in all the later Bibles of the world. These old, old truths have been revamped and presented to the public by gifted minds in countless forms. Many of these forms have been beautiful and of rare literary value. This book aims only at simplicity and practicality in the use of these age-old truths.

It aims to help many, not to please the few. This work is not intended to compete for imperishable honors in the halls of art, but to be here and now a daily help to struggling souls on life's crowded highways.

IV

THE LIFE WORTH WHILE

Like one blindfolded groping out his way,
I will not try to touch beyond to-day.
Since all the future is concealed from sight,
I need but strive to make the next step right.

"THE Life Worth While" differs in the minds of individuals. That which seems worth while to one may seem unendurable to another; and so any analysis of the subject must be made from the purely personal standpoint, and must not be considered an effort to lay down arbitrary laws for the human race to follow.

The religious fanatic in certain parts of India thinks life is worth while if he is enabled to sit in one position for ten years and to suffer physical anguish while he holds his arm above his head in order to prove his willingness to mortify the body. Hundreds of devotees do him reverence, and furnish him with food to sustain life in order that he may continue to suffer; and in this peculiar manner he illustrates his ideal of the life worth while.

The Yogi, who is of a higher order of mind, believes the only life worth while is one devoted to religious communings and to a study of the Creative Powers which caused this universe to come into material expression. He lives much alone, dwells frequently in caves for long periods of time; and comes forth to associate with his kind only as he can cast spiritual light upon life's pathways. He avoids all excesses; he eats merely to sustain life, dresses solely to cover the body from heat or cold, bathes twice a day, never feasts or fasts inordinately, and ignores all mortal aims, ambitions, and occupations.

The inventor in his laboratory, the creator in the world of art or literature in his study, the nun in her cell, the Salvation Army enthusiast in her street concert, the woman of fashion in her opera-box, the financier in adding millions to millions, all feel that they are living the life worth while.

To each one the life of any of the others would be unendurable. So long as there is deep interest, enthusiasm, and pleasure in the life we are living that life must be worth while, even if to the observer it seems frivolous or mistaken. The world is made interesting by its variety of inhabitants, with their varying ideas and occupations. People it with one kind of human beings, all bent on the same object and doing the same kind of work or following the same kind of pleasure, and earth would become intolerably monotonous. Even the frivolous things, the mistaken things, and the wrong things which people do are sometimes worth while, because they lead those who are engaged in them to knowledge of their worthlessness. Looking back along the road of life, many of us can see where we profited by pursuing the wrong trail for a season. We learned that it led to the land of nowhere or into jungles and quagmires, and now we are protected for evermore—in this incarnation or another—from wanting to tread that path.

Not every soul can win the race
  By always running right.
Some feet must tread the mountain's base
  Before they gain the height.

Yet if this consciousness of what is best and right, and wise and true, be born in a man, or bred in him from his cradle to maturity, blest is he that need not learn through his mistakes! But doubly, then, is he blest if with this consciousness dwell sympathy and understanding for those who must learn the lesson otherwise. For sympathy is the keynote to the life worth while.

Most lives contain something which makes them worth while; but once, at least, I have seen a life which seemed to me utterly worthless. An elderly woman, going down into the valley of old age, born to wealth, wedded to one who had given her kindness and devotion, yet living a life of utter selfishness; concerned only with the events of her personal social circle; worrying about her gowns and her menus, stimulating a depleted system to carry her through her petty ambitions, and seeking sleep through the medium of drugs. Yet when this woman was born there was a great rejoicing, for she inherited wealth and an honorable name and every blessing.

Surely no child born in a poor tenement-house or no foundling left upon a doorstep ever made life less worth while than this favorite of fortune. For even upon the verge of the grave she had failed to learn how trivial and petty were her aims and ambitions, and no regret for wasted opportunities touched her atrophied old heart. Such a life must renew itself in a later incarnation, in poverty and loneliness; and, spurred by necessity, it must struggle out into the light of knowledge and learn the blessedness of work and the growth which comes through effort.

My own ideal of the life worth while is one which brings into play all the physical, mental, and spiritual powers inherent in the human being. It includes growth along all of those lines, from the crudeness of adolescence to the maturity of age.

First of all must come a purpose, an object. It may be the cultivation of a talent, it may be the learning of a trade, it may be the accomplishment of some philanthropic aim, or the establishment of an ideal home, or the performance of a duty. But whatever it is, however simple or however great, there must be enthusiasm behind the impulse.

And there must be something more than mere personal aggrandizement or the effort to outshine or outdo some other, or all others, to make it a corner-stone of the life worth while.

With such a purpose in the heart, and a goal in the distance toward which continual effort is directed, there must be a consciousness of the necessity to *be* as well as to *do*, if the life is to be made worth while. So many of us, striving to achieve and to perfect the work we have chosen to do, fail to realize how much more important is the work given us to do by the great Master—the perfecting of character. Should not *that* be considered the real work of a life worth while?

In what I do I note the marring flaw,
  The imperfections of the work I see;
  Nor am I one who'd rather *do* than *be*,
Since its reversal is Creation's law.

Nay, since there lies a better and a worse,
  A lesser and a larger, in men's view,
  I would be better than the thing I do,
As God is greater than his universe.

He shaped Himself before He shaped one world:
  A million eons, toiling day and night,
  He built Himself to majesty and might,
Before the planets into space were hurled.

And when Creation's early work was done,
  What crude beginnings out of chaos came—
  A formless nebula, a wavering flame,
An errant comet, a voracious sun.

And, still unable to perfect His plan,
  What awful creatures at His touch found birth—
  Those protoplasmic monsters of the earth,
That owned the world before He fashioned Man.

And now, behold the poor, unfinished state
  Of this, His latest masterpiece! Then why,
  Seeing the flaws in my own work, should I
Be troubled that no voice proclaims it great?

Before me lies the cycling rounds of years;
  With this small earth will die the thing I do;
  The thing I *am*, goes journeying onward through
A million lives, upon a million spheres.

My work I build, as best I can and may,
  Knowing all mortal effort ends in dust.
  I build myself, not as I may, but must,
Knowing, for good or ill, that self must stay.

Along the ages, out and on, afar,
  Its journey leads, and must perforce be made:
  Likewise its choice, with things of shame and shade,
Or up the path of light, from star to star.

When all these solar systems shall disperse,
  Perchance this labor, and this self-control,
  May find reward, and my completed soul
Will fling in space a little universe.

One who sets himself this task of perfecting his nature, as he goes along toward achievement, will find the analysis of his own motives and the cause of his own actions full of interest and benefit. Are you intent upon erecting a house of many stories? If so, why? Is it to build a mansion taller than your neighbor's and one that shall cause all observers to envy you? Or is it to give comfort and light and fresh air to its inhabitants?

Do you seek wealth? For what, then? Is it to enable you to give expensive dinners, to wear imported garments, and to outshine your comrades in life's journey? Or is it to enable you to make yourself more useful in the world? And are you sufficiently acquainted with your own disposition and sure of your own good sense and will power to be certain that you *would* live the life worth while, and dispense your riches wisely, if you attained your object?

Do you seek fame and glory? For what? That you may be envied and lauded; or that you may develop the best that lies in you, use all your powers, and utilize all your talents; and after you have reached your goal that you may be an influence for good in the world?

Only as we analyze our motives and bring them to the standard where they can meet the clear eyes of our own consciousness can ambition fit into the life worth while.

The man or woman who achieves great things in the mental world and who neglects the body, the health, the personal appearance, cannot live life to its fullness—or perfection.

When we pass from earth we will dispense with this physical body; and as we go through each plane of life we will become more and more ethereal, until at last we are simply luminous, spiritual beings clothed in a body of light.

But until we enter these realms and while we are on earth the physical body deserves our care, our respect, and its measure of our attention. It was created by our thoughts and acts in other incarnations, and has been given us as the result of our own deeds in the past. Whatever it is, we made it so; and it behooves us to take good care of it while here, to refine it by our methods of life, to beautify it by our thoughts, and to keep it clean, strong, and well clothed.

Comely clothing has its part in life, with lovely homes and fair scenery, with graceful furniture and appetizing food. All the material things of this life are meant for our rational enjoyment while we occupy the material body.

To despise them, and to endeavor to live wholly in the spirit, before we are taken out of this realm, is to serve only one part of the school life intended for our development. To live wholly for and in material pleasures is to keep in the primary class of that school and refuse to progress to higher grades. The individual who appreciates the physical and mental sides of existence and takes no interest in spiritual matters can never live the really worth-while life.

Man is a triangle; and he is abnormal if any one side of this triangle is dwarfed. He is like a tree which roots deep into earth and spreads out straggling, wide branches, but does not grow up into the light.

Have you not met the intellectual giant with a strong physique, a bulging brow, and brilliant eye, who scoffed at any idea of life immortal? Or who, if he did not scoff, turned a listless look and an indifferent ear to any remark upon spiritual subjects?

And have you not felt that same shock which accompanies the first sight of a physically deformed human being?

Even when such a person makes no reference to spiritual matters, the finely attuned human being with delicate perceptions misses something from his personality.

Every thought we send from our mind carries with it a certain vibration. Every emotion we conceal in our hearts sends forth its influence. The man who has an awakened consciousness of his own divine inheritance may not speak of it; but he radiates a certain *something* which may be likened to the ultra-violet rays carrying healing and beauty on their beams.

The man who is agnostic, indifferent, or an unbeliever in anything beyond this physical plane of existence cannot radiate this light because he has not provided himself with the spiritual mechanism which produces the violet rays of the soul.

Wealth, education, and position may all enable the individual who is properly equipped otherwise to live the life worth while in a broader and more useful manner than the poor man can live it. But the poor man, the uneducated and humble man, may live that life if he understands the real purpose of existence.

There was a little frail laundress who supported four children and an aged, bedridden mother and a good-natured but weak-willed husband who was a periodical drunkard.

When not in his cups the man was repentant, kindly, affectionate, and appreciative of all the good qualities of his life-mate. So she felt it her duty to bear with him and to regard his failing in the light of a physical malady. The bedridden and complaining old mother was a God-given duty which she must meet with cheerfulness and patience; and her home must be made a place of brightness and merriment and comfort for her growing children.

Without any deep wisdom or formulated ideas this simple woman lived the life worth while in all its beautiful completeness. Her humble tasks she performed with a deep sense of gratitude to her patrons and to her Creator that she was enabled to find employment and to sustain her family. There was always a smile on her face and a bright word of cheer on her lip.

In every factory all over our land there are thousands of good girls possessed of beauty, youth, and all the longings for pleasure and fair apparel which accompanies youth and beauty. These girls are looking temptation in the face daily—

listening to its seductive voice, yet turning away and performing weary and ofttimes distasteful work in order to keep their self-respect and to be worthy of the love and confidence of parents and relatives dependent upon them for support.

Every such work-girl in our great country is living the life worth while. It does not matter what her creed, or how great her lack of education, or how limited her sphere in the world. The fact that she has chosen the rough, right way, and turned her back upon the seemingly smooth, wrong way, because she knew it to be wrong, places her in the ranks of those who are living the life worth while.

I once heard a man bemoaning the fact that he had failed to achieve anything in life. He had missed his early goal; he had not left a name in the world of manly endeavor. Yet this man had in early youth sacrificed personal pleasures and ambitions in order to devote his life to aiding needy relatives. He had made his name blest by the widow and the fatherless; and through his influence and example other lives were bettered and brightened. This man did not know that he had been living the Life Worth While. He imagined that he had failed because he had not carved his name in letters of gold on the temple of Mammon or Fame.

The woman who makes an ideal home for her husband and her children; the man who keeps the flame of love and romance burning in the heart of the wife of his youth (passing by those temptations for adventure in the realm of passion which come to every man); the business man who prefers a clear, clean record and continual need of economy to affluence and graft; the woman who chooses hard work and self-respect before ease and shame—all these and many more, whose simple lives are unknown to the world, are living the life worth while. Viewed from every standpoint, life seems to be worth while.

In this earthly life lie all the elements of beauty, happiness, and growth which the devout minds associate only with the life beyond. For earth is the anteroom of heaven, if we choose to see it so.

V

BEGIN NOW

Love sent me forth, to Love I go again,
For Love is all, and over all. Amen.

IF you are the victim of failure, and are wondering why you have not succeeded as well as many other less deserving people of your acquaintance, it might be well for you to cast a retrospective eye over your past.

It is, of course, more agreeable to lay the blame of all your misfortunes upon Fate; but your future will stand a better chance of being brighter if you discover what part of it lies in yourself and learn how to overcome circumstances and change environment.

Perhaps you started out on the get-rich-quick method of financiering. You made up your mind that old-fashioned ideas of industry and patient labor were all nonsense in this rapid age. You had examples of multimillionaires to offer as arguments when any one doubted your wisdom.

But not every man can be a successful villain, thief, or liar. And the man who undertakes to follow the methods of great robbers on a small scale usually finds himself in prison or out of a position, instead of rich and popular. In the present stage of our evolution the world temporarily admires a big swindler, but it eternally despises a little one.

Better right-about-face and reconstruct your life on a wholly old-fashioned basis of integrity and worth. Perhaps you were meaning to walk the right path, but went astray and fell into the quagmires of error and sin. Now you do not know the way back and feel that it is too late to try and find the path.

But there is never a soul so lost that it cannot get back into Truth's roadway if it cries persistently enough to the sentinels from the Invisible Realms, who stand near to help those who appeal to them.

Keep calling; they will lift you from the quagmire, but you must help yourself at the same time. God's angels help those who help themselves.

Perhaps you have begun ten things and never finished one, and have formed slipshod methods of thought and action, which are the real cause of all your failures.

You can do twenty things after a fashion, and nothing well. Yet you wonder why you have never found your place in the world and why your many capabilities have met with such poor reward.

You may be one of those people who no sooner

begin a piece of work than they are seized with a feverish desire to do something else, and so rush through what they have started to accomplish at breakneck speed, slighting the work in hand for the work in mind.

Or, still worse, you may be a victim of the "By-and-by" and "Time-enough" mottoes.

Alas for the people who are always "going" to do "things"! The Valley of Pretty Soon is white with the bleaching bones of men and women who died while telling how they were *going to do* this and that.

Thought is power, and when thought is spent on the By-and-by instead of being used on the Now, it is as wasteful as to throw gold into the sea instead of sending it into circulation to benefit humanity.

If you have an ambition or purpose in your mind, *act upon it at once.* There is not an hour to waste. *Do something* toward beginning. Rouse yourself from the lethargy of dreams and make a start on facts. It is wonderful what power comes to us after we really begin any undertaking. With every postponement of that beginning, just so much power is dissipated. The road to success lies along the path of Decision, and up the hill of Endeavor, and across the bridge of Patience.

The road to Defeat lies through the Valley of Pretty Soon, and the winding paths of Wait-a-while.

Whatever you intend to do By-and-by begin *NOW.*

VI

THE COMMON-SENSE LEAVEN OF THE LAW

The truest greatness lies in being kind,
The truest wisdom in a happy mind.

THERE was a woman of limited mental powers who listened to lectures on Mental Science and the power of mind, and she decided to develop her child of ten into a wonder of wit and a musical prodigy.

She was utterly lacking in a sense of humor herself, and she had never been able to understand the different major and minor keys or the intricacies of time in music.

She decided to give her son those things she lacked. She put him in the hands of music teachers, and she procured for him all the humorous books she could find in the libraries. Then she devoted an hour in the Silence each day to asserting success for her child.

But the boy was bored with the books; and he was the dullest pupil in music ever known; and after three years his discouraged music-master advised the mother to waste no more money on her son's musical education, but to give him opportunity to develop his taste for athletics. Thereupon the mother decided there was no truth in Mental Science or the theories about the divine power in each soul to be what it willed to be. But the woman had not used good sense.

Wit is a gift, like music, poetry, and painting. A sense of humor lacking, it is difficult to train or direct a mind to see the merry or absurd or comical side of things. It would be impossible to teach a boy born with a mechanical genius to compose oratories or epics. It would be a waste of time to try. Just so it would be folly to try to train the serious or philosophical mind to humor.

Let each human being grow into the best of his own kind. Train him along natural lines—that is the way to educate.

Common sense is quite another thing. It can be cultivated by teachers and parents in children who do not seem to possess it in any degree. *But first the parents and the teachers must possess it*—and few do.

I have seen a dreamy, visionary, improvident, and extravagant boy trained into practical prudence, thrift, and economy by the persistent guidance of an uncle he loved and who loved him. The brain-cells were entirely remade in the course of a few years of constant association with the uncle.

Fear is self-consciousness sometimes, sometimes an anemic condition, sometimes the result of false education. The child that never hears stories about the "dark," who never read "Little Red Riding-hood" and other fear-inciting tales, and who has not been nagged and scolded by its parents in the effort to make it a perfect child, is not liable to feel fear on slight provocation. The old theology with its absurd and blasphemous stories of lakes of hell-fire for the children of unbelievers, and an avenging and frowning God, did much to awaken fear in children and render them nervous and timid.

I have heard mature men describe the nights of horror they passed as little children after listening to one of the old-time sermons and the awful terror of death which such pernicious teachings inculcated. A mother who during the nine months preceding her child's birth lives in fear of poverty or death, or who is in terror of a drunken or cruel or unkind husband, marks her child with a timid and easily frightened nature.

A child of two or three years was given to hours of hysterical weeping without any apparent cause. But the cause lay in the fact that the mother lived with her husband's family and the baby was unwelcome to all, as the father was dependent financially on his parents. Yet such an unfortunate birth-mark can be educated out of the child by a cheerful and kind and wholesome environment.

While the great talents cannot be educated

into a human being, all the unworthy and unfortunate traits *can* be educated *out*, and the great virtues awakened by persistent efforts on the part of associates, guides, and teachers.

A man who wrote good strong prose and who was a devout believer in the power of the will to achieve anything wasted precious time and energy in a determination to be a poet. He studied all the laws governing verse, and he put large, virile ideas into correct mechanical form. Yet he was unable to produce one line of poetry. All he wrote in verse left his readers cold and unstirred; many of his would-be poems jarred like discords in music, even though they "scanned" according to rule. But the divine *something* was not there. He had mistaken his vocation. In our applica- of this great Law, of the power of the Will to achieve results, we must employ reason and logic. We must use this law along the line of least resistance.

Finding where our strongest powers lie, and our best abilities, we should turn our whole intellectual and spiritual batteries in that direction. Think, study, meditate, affirm, pray, and work to attain desired results in the undertaking for which we are fitted by nature. The man who is color-blind and unable to distinguish shades and tones easily may overcome this misfortune to a great degree by patient practice in studying colors. But he should never seek a position on trains or ships, where the observance of signals is an important part of duty; nor should he try to become an artist. In neither field could he gain honors.

Children should be watched as they develop into thinking beings, and their tastes and tendencies should be carefully noted by wise parents and instructors. Then every effort should be made according to old and new thought methods to encourage the growth of the very best qualities and to eliminate by lack of use all undesirable traits and propensities.

By encouraging words and by forceful silent thought vibrations the most unpromising child may be helped to grow into what a wise parent desires. But the *wise* parent never desires the impossible. He does not try to make a mechanic out of a musical prodigy, nor a musical prodigy out of a born mechanic who is tone-deaf. He does not try to produce a Beau Brummel or a dilettante out of an athlete whose nature cries for the open, nor a farmer out of one who is never content save with a book in hand.

Find what your child can best do, what he is best fitted by nature to undertake. Then give him the benefit of your affirmations for success. All New Thought methods should first fit into God's supreme plan. Then they cannot fail.

VII

MODERN MARRIAGE

This ever-growing argument of sex
Is most unseemly and devoid of sense.
Why waste more time in controversy, when
There is not time enough for all of love,
Our rightful occupation in this life?

WHY the contention, the separations, the ever-increasing ratio of divorces that follow the marriages of to-day? In short, what is the matter with the modern marriage?

There is nothing the matter with modern marriage.

The trouble lies with modern men and women.

And there is nothing the matter with modern men and women save growing-pains.

When the boys and girls are suffering from growing-pains they lose the charm of early childhood and display ungraceful and awkward traits; they do not know what to do with their hands and feet; and their manners and attitudes are self-conscious. They are frequently in the way of their elders.

So the men and women who are passing from

early immature social conditions to a higher state are similarly afflicted.

They have lost the old repose of accepted traditions; they are restless with self-consciousness; and their manners and emotions cause them to be in their own way and in the way of others. It is often remarked by the pessimist, who feels that the race is going to the devil, that divorce is a modern evil, and that its frequency to-day proves how the human family in civilized lands has degenerated.

Our grandparents regarded divorce as a disgrace. There was one divorce in their day to a hundred in the present time. But that does not mean that there were ninety-nine happy marriages in those days compared to one in this epoch.

It means that men and women bore their marital unhappiness more patiently and silently in olden times, because it was the custom, and because they dreaded the scandal and reproach which would result if they sought for freedom.

Women especially in the days of our ancestors had not begun to feel growing-pains. They accepted whatever ills fell to their lot in marriage with a certain "Patient Griselda" spirit, believing it to be woman's sphere in life to submit to man's will in all things.

If the man built large, comfortable barns for his stock and housed his horses more luxuriously than his family, if he compelled his wife to do her household work under the most trying conditions, if he was niggardly with his money and humiliated her to the dust by making her beg for every penny she spent on her wearing-apparel, and then complained of her extravagance, she bore it all without an idea of rebelling and told her troubles only to her mother, who advised her to be patient and make the best of her situation.

She had little opportunity to compare her destiny with other lives, as homes were isolated, methods of travel primitive, and newspapers did not lay bare the domestic lives of communities, as in the present day.

Even infidelity on the part of the husband was borne as best it might be in those days, because separation of man and wife left the wife with a stigma upon her for ever. And rather than return to her parents' home, branded and ostracized, she remained in her husband's house and seemed to ignore her humiliating position.

To listen to the prattling of people who delight in lauding the past to the detriment of the present, one would be led to believe that our ancestors were all models of nobility and that the men and women of the present day are degenerate specimens of worthy forebears.

But a little investigation will prove that the sins of omission and commission of our ancestors produced the "divorce-while-you-wait" type of men and women of our own times.

Had the old man never failed in his duty the

new woman would never have sprung into existence. All the one-time domestic virtues of women were taken as a matter of course by the men folk.

Woman's work was in the home, and it was a too generally accepted idea that she was incapable of handling money, and that she needed no diversion, no independent purse, and no mental outlook beyond the walls of her home and the village church.

The type of man who held such ideas prepared the way for the army of suffragists who march through the land to-day.

The Puritan Fathers were merciless in their attitude toward a woman who made a misstep in the path of rectitude, and the two standards of morals, which made light of the sin of the erring youth and damned for ever the erring girl, helped to bring about the revolt of woman against the established order of things.

The silence of mothers on matters of sex has paved a broad highway for unhappy marriages, and now that women are reading, thinking, and observing, they dare to stand forth in the light of Knowledge and demand cleaner, saner, and safer laws to protect them from the evils which the old-fashioned wives endured in silent shame and sorrow.

It has been the boast of senseless and unthinking mothers, backed by selfish and uncomprehending fathers, that their daughters went to the marriage altar "as ignorant and innocent in mind as new-born babes" in matters of sex. It would be just as sensible to boast that a school-teacher went to her duties ignorant of reading and writing or a musician ignorant of notes. The misery, the destruction to health and happiness, the wretchedness which has gone into the second and third generations through this ignorance of girl wives and mothers regarding the natural laws which govern marriage and motherhood would fill volumes if written out even in short-hand.

The silence of fathers toward their sons on these great laws of life has aided and abetted the natural selfishness and sensuousness of the masculine nature in sex relations, and the fact that until within a comparatively short period of time all physicians were men has been another factor in the building of conditions which in their time inevitably produced revolt.

The report of the "Committee of One Hundred" on health, together with the statistics of the Board of Health of New York and other states, compels the most optimistic mind to realize the menace to the national conservation of vitality which lies in the ignorance of men and women in matters of sex hygiene.

When men are educated in early youth to understand the importance of keeping the blood pure and the body and mind clean, in order to produce sane, strong children who are mentally and physically a credit to the race, there will be a notable reduction in divorces, and wives and offspring will find less and less need of the surgeon's and physician's skill.

Every day divorces are being granted to wives for all sorts of causes, which, if truthfully stated, would be from one cause only—the vile and promiscuous habits of the husband before marriage and after.

And every day women are sacrificed on the surgeon's table and little children are born blind, scrofulous, and demented from the same causes. Men do not go wilfully and knowingly into these detestable states. They do not with open eyes and minds seek to become moral and physical lepers. It is all the result of silent parents and silent physicians.

Men must be educated in eugenics; they must be taught the great law of self-control, and they must understand the high meaning of the words husband and father. Then we will find marriage growing to be a success and divorce an obsolete word. Together with this all-important education of men, women must be made to cultivate the unusual virtue of common sense before marriage will reach an absolute condition of success.

The failings of men which lead to divorce are usually of a glaring nature, of such a nature that he who runs may read. Drunkenness, or the overuse of intoxicants, which destroy the reasoning powers and the judgment; infidelity and all its ramifications of disease; violent temper; laziness and failure to provide for a family—these are the main chapters in the book of masculine offenses against happy homes. But the offenses of wives are so frequently subtle and elusive, and so veiled from the public eye, that only those who live in the closest relations may discover them.

They are little foxes in the vines and parasites in the trees.

The American girl is almost invariably a spoiled child before she reaches adolescence.

She rules her father and mother, and her brothers wait upon her. She is virtually the head of the house, and her wish is law and her whims are like royal edicts. If she marries the spoiled son of a fond mother it is a case of Greek meeting Greek, and discord must ensue. And if she marries an unselfish and worshiping husband, she often forgets that there is such a thing as the turning of a crushed worm, and imposes upon his patience and kindness and unselfishness until he walks forth to meet her only in the divorce court.

Yet the weapons she has used in slaying Cupid have been concealed from all eyes save her husband's or other eyes under her roof. And the undiscerning public is more than liable to believe she is the injured party when the divorce occurs.

The passion of many women for hotel life, for excitement, and for display amounts to a disease.

It is, perhaps, the swinging of the pendulum from the dull and dreary monotony which characterized the lives of their foremothers. The women of this generation are in many ways suffering from a sort of hysteria caused by the suppression of the emotional natures of their mothers and grandmothers. Just as sons of clergymen do to excess, frequently, everything which their fathers refused to do in reason.

The grandmothers and mothers who lived only to work and make the home comfortable for the men folk produced, by the crucifixion of all natural desires for pleasure and amusement, as descendants a race of women pleasure-seekers. But in his taste for home life man changes little. He is the same in every generation. And the woman who wants to make the man she marries happy needs to understand this fact; and whatever else she may ask of him, to give him first the foundation of a comfortable, beautiful, well-ordered, and attractive home, where even the transient guest can feel the atmosphere of well-being and content. This can be made only by the mental emanations of its inhabitants.

A woman who sets forth in married life determined to make a real wife and mother has chosen the most wonderful and fascinating career it is possible for her to pursue, and its scope is as wide as the universe. To create such a home and magnetize it with the love and enjoyment of a good woman's mind is to prepare an anteroom for heaven.

Many a man inclined to stray into forbidden folds and to seek unwholesome associations would linger in this anteroom were it provided for him by love and good sense, in place of his being forced into the unnatural surroundings of hotels.

Petty jealousies of wives, hampering a good-hearted man in his impulses toward his relatives and near friends, are ofttimes causes of divorces. A man has been known to marry for love (as men usually do) and to set forth with every intention of being a fair and kind and just husband; but before many months he found his relatives, his men comrades, and even his books and domestic pets objects of a small-minded woman's nagging jealousy. And Cupid was driven out of doors, never to return.

Unreasonable extravagance of women is another cause of disaster to the marital association; and this propensity drives many a good-hearted man whose great desire is to please his wife into dishonesty and double dealing in business matters.

Behind prison doors to-day men are serving long sentences who sinned first through weakness and over-devotion to the whims of selfish and unthinking wives. The indolent wife, who settles down lazily into the comfort of a good home, satisfied with the fact that she is married to a man who loves her and unconscious that she must make an effort to keep her husband in love, is another likely candidate for the divorce court.

In our own time and clime ninety-nine men

of each hundred like to feel proud of their wives. They enjoy seeing them look well and regret to observe the effect of time upon their beauty. The woman who does not try to keep herself attractive and who allows self-indulgence and indolence to destroy her figure and complexion is inviting unhappiness to come into her home.

In this busy age, when trains, ships, telegraphs, and telephones keep the whole world in touch, men are aware of the existence of women who understand the art of defying time and who remain attractive despite the passing of years. Even in remote country places men have ceased to regard old age for the matron as a necessity. They realize there is something lacking in the temperament of a woman who lets herself go merely because she is a wife and a mother.

Since men view the subject in this light, the wise woman will not permit her husband to feel ashamed of her. She will think of the art of preservation of her charms as one of her sacred duties, and she will regard the gymnasium and the study of physical culture and the practice of mental calisthenics with respect close to reverence. In the new life which has come to women in the past generation there lies a danger of becoming too absorbed in personal pursuits to keep in touch with the tastes and ambitions of the husband—even to lose all interest in them.

It is well for husband and wife to have their separate occupations and to follow separate tastes and pleasures to a certain degree. But that degree must never lead to diverging interests and must never leave the husband feeling solitary and without the companionship or sympathy of the wife, either in his business or his amusements; nor must the wife be left to find sympathy or admiration elsewhere than at home.

Since the home is the foundation of the nation, it is well worth while for individuals who establish homes to make some personal sacrifice of time and impulses to create a solid rock bed for that foundation.

The lover finds it easy to show an interest in the most frivolous or feminine accomplishment of his lady-love, to admire her embroidery, to listen to her singing, or to help her fit up her booth for a charity bazaar. And whatever she says or does wins his attention. Why not continue that attitude after marriage and give the wife the happy sense of copartnership in all her doings?

Every wife, as a rule, is ready to be taught something of her husband's business or professional affairs, enough to make her understand his ambitions and sympathize with his trials; but it is only the occasional wife who has the perception to understand the delicate difference between sympathizing and interfering with a man's affairs. Perhaps it is because of this danger of interference that so few men make their wives acquainted with their business lives. And this is a point on which women need training. A tactful man can so train the woman he loves, before marriage, by praise of other women who have shown the art of helping their husbands by the right attitude of mind and the right methods of action. Surely there is nothing too much trouble, nothing too time-taking, which may lead to a successful marriage! It is the important work of the human race. For what is the worth of successful art or successful business, what is the worth of peace, power, and prosperity in a nation, what is the use of international arbitration unless that nation is founded on happy, clean, harmonious homes?

One danger which menaces the American native proper (the unmixed American) and menaces happy home life is the alarming tendency of the present generation to avoid parentage.

Young married people in good health, with good brains and bodies to transmit to offspring, resort to even criminal methods of prevention, and wives who might be the proud mothers of statesmen or beautiful daughters in the days to come remain barren wilfully and frequently impair their health and beauty rather than accept the responsibilities of motherhood.

Here again we find the reflex action of mind; for often these wives are daughters of mothers who have borne too many children and have missed the happiness of youth and the relaxation a perfect home should give in the never-ceasing cares of a large family. I do not know what the statistics state regarding the relative number of divorces among childless people and those who are parents, but I do know that Nature intended marriage to be followed by parentage as naturally as summer follows spring. And I know that even the sad experience of a motherhood which lasts but a few brief hours often makes a new and indescribably sacred bond of affection between a husband and wife. There are many happy marriages where no children are, it is true, yet the wife who has never felt the stirring of a little being under her heart has missed one of life's and love's most wonderful experiences.

VIII

THE GENEROUS YEARS

Time cannot take
My three great jewels from the crown of life—
Love, sympathy, and faith: and year on year
He sees them grow in luster and in worth,
And glowers by me plucking at his beard
And dragging as he goes a useless scythe.

JUST as you think of the years, just as you make use of them, so will be their attitude toward you.

Realize first of all that you are greater than the years, greater than time, greater than eternity, because you are part of the vast cause which made them all.

Realize next that the years have accumulated wisdom, power, and knowledge of health, beauty, wealth, and happiness, and that your part lies in winning from them the laws governing these things.

So long as you regard time as a cruel monopolist who will wrest from you all your dearest possessions and give you nothing in return, you are preparing the way for such fears to materialize.

But it rests with you to make the years generous and benevolent instead of grasping and cruel.

The years may be compared to droves of wild horses. If you fly in terror before them they will trample you under their feet, but if you tame and harness them they will carry your chariot to the summit of success.

Again, we may think of them as adepts and masters, dwelling in the temple of life, ready to impart their wisdom to those who come reverently to them, those who bring patience and faith in the search for eternal truths.

It has been the custom of the foolish world for ages to think, talk, and write of beauty, joy, and happiness as pertaining only to early youth.

This same foolish and mistaken world has educated woman in the idea that each year after her first score comes to her as an enemy—a highwayman—bent upon robbing her of all she holds most precious.

It has taught man to regard as a limited one his period of mental and physical prowess; and so these false and unwholesome traditions have helped to hurl the race into premature decay and death.

The wise individual faces each year with expectancy and courage, mingled with reverence, yet with an inner consciousness of superiority.

Expectancy of new revelations of life, courage to meet whatever comes, reverence for the accumulated wisdom which the years carry, and a sense of superiority through the knowledge that mankind is the highest expression of the creative power yet evolved, and the possession of a thinking brain and a loving heart place him in the rank with the lords of the universe.

On her birthday morning every woman should talk with the year which is coming as with a friend who is crossing her threshold to bring her gifts. Let her say, "Oh, Year, I welcome you. Let me come close to you; let me walk beside you and listen to all the secrets which you keep in your great soul for my sharing. You can teach me the divine laws of health, beauty, peace, usefulness, and consequent happiness. You can teach me order and system in all my ways. You can impress upon me the power which comes through the exercise of patience, the strength which results from cold rains and biting frosts, the pleasure which lies in giving of my bounty to others, and the dignity and pride which accompany the preparation of beautiful and appropriate apparel for each season.

"If I breathe in your pure airs, if I live according to those natural laws which govern you, if I accept the spring, the summer, the autumn, the winter of life as perfect expressions of God's bounty, then I, too, may grow in beauty and charm and opulence as the year grows. You have come to teach me these truths; you have come to help me; and I will be richer and happier from your association. And I will be able to understand your laws of perpetual rejuvenation and to illustrate them."

Each man should welcome the year which adds maturity to his life as a teacher who has come to instruct him in power and knowledge of the deeper meanings of existence. He should expect to grow in strength and worth and to make a nobler example of his life with the passing of each twelve months.

Those who face the years with such resolutions, and who determine to be the recipients, not the losers, in their encounter with Time, will find life growing richer and more interesting as they pass from early youth into maturity and from maturity into the still larger field of vision afforded as they climb the western hill.

For the last earthly journey is not a descent, but a climb, for those who take toll from the years instead of paying it.

We should not talk of going down into the valley of death or old age.

We should stand upon the summit of a hill from where we behold the world we have traversed and the shining peaks of the world beyond, whither we are going.

Expect much of the years. Then set yourself to work to aid those years in giving you what you expect.

Do you desire health? Think of the year as charged with health, and use all the opportunities it affords you to breathe deeply the fresh air it offers and sustain yourself with its fresh fruits and vegetables and its wholesome beverages. Keep your mind and your body clean; keep every muscle and organ active and free from impurities; let no part of yourself become sluggish or atrophied from lack of use. Believe health is your divine right, and declare it is yours every hour in the day.

Do you desire beauty? Then declare beauty and think and talk of beautiful things and perform beautiful deeds. Refuse to dwell upon ugliness in any form. Study the needs of your body, and reform such portions as do not please your sense of beauty. Call in such aids as science and hygiene have provided for the accomplishment of your purpose.

Clothe yourself in accordance with your enlarged understanding of the laws of beauty; and always remember that the body is only the casket of the inner jewel, and let your spirit, the divine gem, shine through the casket and create a radiance about you wherever you go.

Do you desire opulence? Then think opulence; be large in your affections; give freely of good will, of praise, of appreciation, of helpful words and acts. Never allow yourself to begrudge another what has come to him; never disparage another's achievements. Let your mind be planted with seeds of love and joy and hope, and courage and universal good will, and opulent harvests shall grow therefrom. Think of each year as a sower scattering these seeds in your heart; then water with the dews of sympathy and throw open the windows to the broad sunlight of heaven while they ripen. And as surely as the days come and go so surely shall your life grow in opulence, spiritual and material. "Seek ye first the kingdom of heaven, and all other things shall be added."

Sorrow may be—nay, must be—the portion some of the years bring you. But, understood and accepted as the working out of a divine law, with a holy purpose, strength, power, and an enlarged vision will be given you through this experience.

There is no greater beautifier in life than a sorrow borne with reverent understanding and accepted in that spirit.

Let us meet the coming years with an invocation.

Oh, wonderful years, share with me your understanding of life; impress upon my mortal mind the beauty of temperate living, the joy of useful labor, the efficacy of applied thought, the revealing miracles of prayer.

Lead me to the Great Source from which comes your eternal youth, undying beauty, vital force, and creative powers. Help me to claim my own; to share with others all that is mine, and to make life on earth a growing glory until I pass onward to other realms. Amen.

IX

TO YOUNG MEN

God chooses His own leaders in the world,
  And from the rest He asks but willing hands.
As mighty mountains into place are hurled,
  While patient tides may only shape the sands.

The weight of an eagle's body is many times greater than that of the air on which it flies. It, therefore, naturally gravitates toward the earth.

Under the laws of gravity it would, if left alone, naturally fall to the ground, never to rise again. But this monarch of the air has the power within itself, and of its own right, to overcome the force of gravity and rise at will to realms beyond the clouds and the shadows of earth, into the clear sunlight of heaven.—From *The Great Psychological Crime.*

YOU have your own night-key, young man, and you are your own master.

No one asks where you are going or at what hour you will return.

You do as you please.

And if it pleases you to "see life" and "know the world," you consider it nobody's business.

It is a part of every man's education, you say.

And even if you plant a crop of wild oats, that,

too, you believe to be included in your Life School Curriculum.

Every protest made you consider "preaching."

But have you never observed that life itself is a great preacher?

Life and Father Time are two great moralists.

Even when they seem to be laughing comrades, helping you sow your crop of "oats," they are sneering at you secretly and waiting the hour when they can talk to you on the benefits of morality and right living.

The Great Creative Power which made the Universe, and systems of universes, gives each human being certain nervous forces and vital qualities.

Properly used, these qualities and forces can make man almost Godlike in his mental, physical, and spiritual strength.

Just as a large fortune properly managed and saved can accomplish miracles in the way of usefulness when rightly applied.

But if that fortune is dissipated day by day, month by month, year by year, its possessor eventually finds himself a pauper.

Precisely so the virile man finds himself a pauper, and worse than a pauper, if he begins sowing his wild oats and "seeing life" and "knowing the world" according to the standards set by the devotees of Folly.

Look about you and take mental notes of middle-aged men who have led the life you are living.

You will see gray faces, or blotched and bloated ones; eyes dull and lifeless, or glaring with the brilliancy of stimulants; and bodies which should be in their prime crippled with disease or shapeless with self-indulgence.

Look farther and learn something of the condition of the children of these men.

Among them you will find the crippled, the blind, the idiotic, the deaf and dumb, the weaklings, and the insane.

And were the family physicians of these men to tell you all they know you would lie awake with horror, wondering how the impression has gone abroad that men can sin and pay no penalty; that woman alone pays for her errors.

Woman does pay a big price; not only for her own sins of the senses, but she pays also for the sins of her lover or her husband.

Our asylums for the insane and our homes for incurables are half filled with women and children who have paid the price for the men who believed it was nobody's business if they chose to "see life" and "know the world."

When a woman makes a wrong step in this direction her punishment usually is swift, and the world knows of it.

A man's punishment is frequently long delayed, but when it comes it demands interest on all the time which has elapsed. Many young and middle-aged men you see walking with canes and crutches, and paying large commissions to physicians to say they have "rheumatism" and "neuritis" and other commonplace maladies, are victims of their own vices. They have "seen life" as you are seeing it.

Look at the faces of men in fashionable clubs; how many of these men are, at forty or fifty or sixty, types which seem admirable to you?

You are young, in the morning of life; before you waste your splendid youth and prepare yourself to be a physical pauper at middle life stop and think of these things a bit.

And consider what qualities and propensities and what kind of blood you are preparing to give your unborn children.

No doubt it is your intention to give them a pure-minded and clean-bodied mother.

But what sort of a father will they have?

When you tell me that you are so dominated by inherited tendencies and mortal passions and appetites, and so surrounded by temptations that you cannot overcome circumstances and make a man of yourself, I ask you to read the above extract and to ponder upon it.

Are you the self-confessed inferior of the eagle? Can you not overcome the law of inheritance or environment, which you say is keeping you from rising, and mount over circumstances and attain your goal? You tell me you have no wings; that the eagle is provided with the mechanism which enables him to soar from low to high places, while you are cumbered with a body of appetites and passions which link you to earth.

But never yet were there wings of birds so strong and mighty as the wings of the will of man; never were there heights so lofty for the feathered creature to seek as those which await the mind of man, once he spreads the pinions of his will and rises from the level places to the summits.

Begin to-day to unfold these pinions.

Relinquish some habit which you know in your secret heart is harmful, but which you believe you have not strength to overcome.

It may be drink, it may be cigarettes, it may be drugs or extravagance or idleness or sensuality or a gross appetite or gambling; it may be a vacillating, changeable mind or a morbid depression that borders on melancholia, or fear and self-consciousness and a lack of self-reliance which prevents you from attempting any new venture; but whatever your besetting sin is you know, and you can rise over it as the eagle rises over the law of gravity and attains the mountain's peak. Unless you do unfold the hidden wings of your will and rise you must go lower in the human scale than you stand to-day.

There is no such thing as standing still in this world. Each soul is either a little stronger or a little weaker, a little nobler or a little less noble, a little more self-reliant or a little more dependent to-day than it was yesterday.

The same process of change will take place to-morrow, and the next day, and the next. You may not be conscious of it, but the friends who saw you last year and see you now after an interval of months are able to say whether you have gone forward or backward in the way of character.

They would not like to tell you so, perhaps, but they know. These things show in your exterior appearance and in your deportment.

You are young, and the world is before you, but do not make the mistake of thinking there is time enough ahead for improvement. Each day the task will become a little more difficult. Each day your besetting weakness will be harder to overcome. Each day the heights will recede and seem more difficult of attainment. And each day your will's unused wings will grow more inert.

Unfold them to-day.

Like a newly fledged bird, try only short flights at first. Do not expect to make the mountain summit in your first attempt. And even if you fail once or twice do not be discouraged. I have seen young birds fall over and over again, but finally soar beyond my vision. Fight away the thoughts of fear, doubt, and despondency which will flock about you at times like swarms of vicious insects. They belong to the marshy places, and after you rise higher they will leave you.

There is a God of love, and you are His expression. You are divine, and your nature is all love and strength and power. Doubt and despondency are serious hindrances to the use of these qualities.

A young man, scarcely more than a lad, says of an enterprise he has in mind: "I mean to get ahead of all rivals in the same line of endeavor."

I do not like this phrase, or the idea it involves. No man or woman should harbor the ambition to "get ahead" of others in mental, moral, or purely business matters. Where there is contest of physical powers, a swimming, running, or jumping race, the expression is well enough; but outside of such tests there are higher qualities to be considered in the effort toward achievements.

In trades, in the professions, and in the arts there is never an exact method of procedure or an exact result which places these occupations on a level with physical sports. Individuality always enters into the success of any man in his life vocation, be that what it may. The one thing to consider in any occupation undertaken *is the best and most complete development of individuality.*

Instead of lying awake nights and planning ways to "get ahead" of competitors, devote yourself to the development of your best abilities, your most original powers, and your highest aspirations.

"Get ahead of yourself," not of some rival.

If you have a shop or an office next door to a competitor, wish him good fortune and say a word for him when occasion demands, and to yourself say, "Whoever comes into this place of business shall receive the best treatment and the most courteous attention in my power to give."

X

MORBIDITIS

When love, health, happiness, and plenty hear
  Their names repeated over day by day,
They wing their way like answering fairies near,
  Then nestle down within our homes to stay.

THE conceited girl or woman is tiresome and unpleasant as a companion, but the morbidly discontented woman is far worse. Perhaps you have met her, with her eternal complaint of the injustice of Fate toward her.

She feels that she is born for better things than have befallen her; her family does not understand her; her friends misjudge her; the public slights her.

If she is married she finds herself superior to her husband and to her associates. She is eternally longing for what she has not; and when she gets the thing craved for she no longer cares for it. It has come too late, she says. The sorrowful side of life alone appeals to her. This she believes is due to her "artistic nature." The injustice of Fortune and the unkindness of society are topics

5

dear to her heart. She finds her only rapture in misery.

If she is religiously inclined she looks toward heaven with more grim satisfaction in the thought that it will strip fame, favors, and fortune from the unworthy than because it will give her the benefits she feels she deserves. She does not dream that she is losing years of heaven here upon earth by her own mental attitude. We build our heavens thought by thought.

If you are dwelling upon the dark phases of your destiny and upon the ungracious acts of Fate, you are shaping more of the same experience for yourself here and in realms beyond. You are making happiness impossible for yourself upon any plane. In your own self lies Destiny.

I have known a woman to keep her entire family despondent for years by her continual assertions that she was out of her sphere, misunderstood and unappreciated. The minds of sensitive children accepted these statements and grieved over "poor mother's" sad life until their own youth was embittered. The morbid mother seized upon the sympathies of her children like a leech and sapped their young lives of joy.

The husband grew discouraged and indifferent under the continual strain, and what might have been a happy home was a desolate one, and its memory is a nightmare to the children to-day.

Understand yourself and your divine possibilities, and you will cease to think you are misunderstood. It is not possible to misunderstand a beautiful, sunny day. All nature rejoices in its loveliness. Give love, cheerfulness, kindness, and good will to all humanity, and you need not long worry about being misunderstood. Give the best you have to each object, purpose, and individual, and you will eventually receive the best from humanity.

I doubt if a human being lives, no matter how seemingly fortunate and to be envied, who could not find a whole chapter of miseries to mourn over if he or she chose to turn over the leaves of Life's book to that particular page. In every life there is always something which might be bettered.

One person likes his environment, but hates his occupation; another likes his work, but dislikes his environment; one wants the city; another wants the country; and so on *ad infinitum.*

You feel you are particularly unfortunate in not having a harmonious home, in not having more companionship with people who are congenial, and in having a great many material worries.

You carry always a face of sorrow and a look of sadness; and you tell me life grows more and more a very serious thing to you. You are meantime forgetting that you are blest with health; that you are in possession of all your faculties; that you are not crippled or bedridden; and that you are pursuing an occupation which you like.

You breathe good fresh air in your home; you are not shut up in a tenement house; you are not confined in a factory all day; and you are not starved for good food.

Why, my dear girl, with such a list of things which could make life hard indeed for one left out of what Fate gives you it seems to me your days should be one pæan of thanks to God and one prayer for voice and words to praise Him for His manifold blessings.

An inharmonious home is indeed a great trouble; but the only thing for one to do who suffers from such a cause is to *be one note of harmony in the discords*.

Speak the silent word of love to each member of the family; say "Peace, be still" to the troubled domestic ocean, and by every thought, word, and act set the example of harmony. Miracles have been wrought by one loving, patient soul in a home of many wrangling minds. Refuse to quarrel; refuse to be sullen; refuse to be sarcastic; and by the example of love and kindness and good cheer shame the other members of the household into better behavior.

Then, if they continue to be disagreeable, speak the word of *freedom* to your own soul; and picture to yourself a life apart from the family. It will come to you if you live in a way deserving of this freedom. It will come either by a change in the people who make the discord or in your change to other surroundings. It can never come while you are pitying yourself. Self-pity is weakness and a waste of mental force. It is a great weakness of character to continually crave pity and sympathy and to want people to be sorry for you.

Just as well might every pupil who is given a lesson ask all the teachers and all the other scholars to be "sorry" and bestow sympathy. We are placed in this world where our actions and thoughts in other lives direct our path; and we are here to build character and learn the power which lies in our minds to change present conditions and shape a better future. We can never do this by constantly mourning over our situation. For such feelings waste our energies and prevent constructive processes of thought.

Begin right now, to-day, my dear girl, to thank God for whatever has come to you; thank Him for trouble and sorrow; and ask Him to show you the way to transmute these things into a strong, helpful, character, and to give you the power to work up and out of all conditions which are distasteful to you. This is your work; and you alone can do it. Then look about you for things to rejoice over, and think and talk of these, and allow no one to be sorry for you.

Stand before your mirror and laugh every day for five minutes; and when you feel the corners of your mouth turning down bring them up—and laugh again.

And before very long you will discover that you are no longer to be pitied, but to be congratulated.

For you will have made a new heaven and a new earth for yourself.

XI

PRENATAL INFLUENCE

God loved so much, His thoughts burst into flame,
And from that sacred Source creation came.

THERE is nothing we cannot hope for for future generations once men and women are awakened to a realization of what prenatal influence means.

Six or seven years ago a discouraged and troubled woman wrote to a friend of her misfortunes. The husband was out of employment, there were five children to feed and clothe and another child coming.

"How can I be glad of this child or feel anything but despair at the thought of bringing another being into this troubled life?" she asked. "How can I give my unborn offspring prenatal influences for anything but sorrow?"

"Try," urged the friend, in reply. "Face the inevitable with a courage which shall compel the respect of the unseen presences always about us. Select some picture which pleases you and look upon it often, thinking you would like your child to resemble it. Select some character in history, and then from your neighborhood library obtain books about that character, and read and think of the qualities which your child may acquire by your efforts. Focus your mind upon this subject. Whenever you become melancholy use your will power, and say to yourself that the Creator of all life is great and good enough to care for you and protect you through your trial, and that the work for you to do is to mold your child into a beautiful character and to fit it for a comfort and joy to yourself and humanity. You are building something which will mean good or evil for the world for time and eternity. You are bringing into existence a *human being.*

"Such a colossal thought ought to take such complete possession of you that nothing petty, nothing gloomy, nothing selfish, nothing less than greatness and glory could enter your mind.

"That child now under your heart has lived many times before on earth. It will come with many impulses and tendencies brought over from old incarnations, and many others from your own ancestors and those of the father. *But greater than all these impulses and tendencies is the mind of the mother to mold and shape that child into what it will be.* If you realize how wonderful is the work given to do, and how far-reaching will be the results of how you do it, a great awe will fall upon you, with a great exultation.

"You will fall on your knees and lift your face

to the Invisible Helpers, and cry out: 'Creator, God, and all Holy Angels and Intelligences in the world and systems of worlds about and beyond me, help me to be worthy of this mighty mission of motherhood with which I am charged. Thrill me, stir me, enlighten me with wisdom; give me light and guidance; and show me the way to give to the world a perfect child.'

"This prayer will be from the depths of your being, and it will be repeated every day, and you will fall asleep at night with the words on your lips.

"Then you will guard yourself from all evil thinking or speaking, from gloomy or depressing thoughts; because you will know that one who so respects the mission intrusted to her and who so believes in her great responsibility will be guarded and helped over all the hard places by the Divine Guides, who are ever about us.

"You will avoid looking at the ugly, the deformed, or the repulsive things of earth. You will read no tales of crime and allow no one to talk such things to you, because you will not want to pass on to your unborn child anything but the beautiful, healthful, and inspiring things of life.

"You will read good books, biographies of noble lives, accounts of brave and noble deeds; and you will listen to sweet music, and go into churches and galleries and see beautiful pictures, or walk in woods and fields and look at lovely nature. And always will there be the prayer and the faith in your heart that brings the Invisible Helpers near. You will believe that a Great Soul is coming to earth, through you, a soul that will be helpful and happy, and that will bring the best joy into your own life that it has ever known. And with all your heart and mind and mental and spiritual powers you will love this baby hidden away under your heart; and you will be brave and courageous and know that all must be well with you and it. For of such is the Kingdom of Heaven."

Meantime the friend sent the burdened mother books and letters to cheer her and made such effort as was in her power to obtain work for the father and clothing and fuel for the family.

Recently the friend received a letter from the mother saying what changes the years had brought to the family. The husband and father has a good position, and by careful economy they are able to satisfy the actual needs of the eight members of the household and to pay a small sum each week to liquidate their debts. And the baby which was the cause of such despondency and almost despair to the expectant mother is the glory and joy of the household. Already the child seems to radiate sunlight and hope and to show unusual beauty and attractiveness.

"Poor as we still are," the mother writes, "my heart is full of joy all day long over our improved condition, and the control I learned to exercise over my mind those months and the lesson I learned of my ability to drive away melancholy and invite cheerfulness have been worth all they cost me."

Time alone can tell just what will be the result of the mother's concentrated effort to make her child an ideal character, but surely the present results are so gratifying to this mother that they should encourage thousands of other women similarly situated who read this little story. Every expectant mother should feel it her first great duty to control and guide her mind toward some desirable ideal, no matter how difficult her position may be.

Every good thought and impulse, every kind feeling and sweet act cultivated, every unworthy mood and rebellious thought governed at such a time means a work done for eternity. A woman who has lived to see her son reflect every mood of her mental condition before his birth writes to-day that she feels her work in the future lies in giving talks to girls and women upon this all-important subject.

"Before my son was born," she writes, "a relative asked me if I knew the power of mental prenatal influence. I had been reared by a 'modest' mother, one of the old-fashioned kind, who had taught me that to mention an unborn child was indelicate. Oh, the misfortune such mothers have entailed upon their children! I was indignant at the relative who referred to my condition, and of course lost an opportunity to benefit by her knowledge. Not until I lived to see my own uncontrolled moods reflected in my child, and to suffer for the injury I had done him when he was helpless to defend himself, did I awaken to the wonder and majesty and terror of prenatal conditions. 'And now I am going to do what I can to make other women realize their power to mold their children to be what they desire."

This is a great work for any woman to undertake, and may success and joy attend her.

XII

THE NEGLECTED ART OF GOOD PARENTHOOD

Love much. There is no waste in freely giving;
He who loves much alone finds life worth living:
Love on, through doubt and darkness; and believe
There is no thing which Love may not achieve.

ARE you a parent of grown children?

If so, just what do you know of their methods of enjoyment outside the home, or even at home?

Do you take a sympathetic interest in all their pleasures, and do you try to make them feel you are their friend, and that you have not forgotten your own youth?

Are they on such happy terms with you that they tell you all their little secrets and talk over all their hopes and ambitions and longings? Have you made your own son feel respect and a high sense of responsibility toward all women? Does he understand that sex relations are sacred matters and that any light or low view of the subject is fraught with enormous dangers for him and for his descendants? Unless a young man knows this, from the scientific and medical side, he is not well equipped to go about seeking for social pleasures in safety. He is in danger himself, and he is liable to become a menace to those with whom he associates.

Has your young daughter any knowledge of herself as a woman and a possible mother of another generation, which will protect her from disaster, morally or physically? Possibly, being your daughter, you feel she must be safe from doing any foolish or wrong act. But you must remember how many other ancestors have given her tendencies and qualities and impulses of which you know nothing.

First and foremost she is a human being, a part of nature, and she will pass through the same stages of development which flowers and plants and animals pass through. Just as the tree buds and then flowers and then bears fruit, so every normal woman experiences these instincts to carry on nature's work. But as she cannot perform these functions as naturally and frankly as the things in the vegetable and animal kingdom do, she needs guidance and protection through the romantic bud and flower periods of her unfoldment. Tendencies which an unkind and undiscriminating world might call evil are simply natural tendencies for mating and bearing offspring. They show themselves in romantic impulses and a desire to enjoy the society of the opposite sex.

That desire should be gratified, but it should be guided and protected. Are you protecting your daughter? Do you know what hours she keeps with her callers; and when she visits her girl friends, do you know what places they visit and who are their escorts, and what hour she reaches her rooms?

If you are the parents of small children, are you giving them any foundation of good manners and agreeable behavior and kindly instincts which will make them tractable students when they begin to attend school and will cause the tendrils of their young minds to reach up to lovely qualities, instead of trailing down into the dust of selfishness and the mire of immorality? The most important duties of parenthood are often cast on the burdened shoulders of teachers.

Having brought a child into the world and to a school age is not all of the responsibility of a father and mother. Not even when accompanied by generosity and a willingness to pay teachers to do the work neglected at home. Nothing can ever quite recompense a child who has reached the age of ten without having received the loving, careful training of a patient mother or father in the small, gracious things which make up daily conduct.

Any parent, however poor, can teach a child to speak low, to avoid flat contradictions, to be respectful to elders, to sit correctly, to partake of food silently, and enter and leave a room gracefully.

Did you ever know how the story came to be told children that the stork brings the little brothers and sisters to the household?

It seems that the stork is very much devoted to its young, and also most affectionate to its older progeny.

In southern Europe and Egypt the storks are much loved and protected. They build their nests in chimneys or in old ruins or church spires. The Father Stork is devoted to his family and supplies food for the young in the nests, and he and Mother Stork are very careful to keep the birdies in their nests till they are quite strong enough to learn to fly. When they can safely fly, they start with their parents to warmer lands. In Holland some people build nests on the house-tops to induce the storks to come. People would rather build a new chimney than disturb a stork's nest, as they are considered great good luck to have near; and, as almost all people in those lands think large families are a blessing, the belief grew up that having the devoted Stork parents building nests on the roof brought them the happiness of a large family.

"Modest" parents declare they want to keep their children "innocent" and ignorant of all things pertaining to those subjects just as long as possible; and many a proud mother is heard declaring her daughter of seventeen is as innocent as a babe unborn.

But such innocence is criminal on the part of the parent.

Besides, it is seldom true.

The mother is deceived.

Few children go through one primary term in public school and remain ignorant of these subjects. But their knowledge is gained from low sources usually, and their minds are tarnished by having to receive the instruction in a vulgar or unwholesome manner.

It is the mother's place to talk to her children and to tell them just as many of life's great truths as their young minds can assimilate, and then to impress upon them the dignity and good form of silence on these subjects. When a mother makes her child a confidant in this way she wraps it about with a mantle of purity and protection which no rude hand can tear away.

All the fathers and mothers in America who believe themselves to be in any way decent and respectable people continually deplore the prevalence of graft, dishonesty, and every form of thievery in our land. And yet not one pair of parents in ten bring up little children with careful, high ideals respecting the rights and property of their neighbors and their associates. It is during the first ten years of a child's life that such ideals must be formed in order to become a part of the character. An especially bright, intellectual boy of ten years of age was heard commenting, with regret, on the dishonesty of American politics. He declared his opinion that all politicians were thieves, pocketing the money which belonged to the people for their own use. Yet the very same day this small boy had stopped by the roadside and picked flowers from a garden which belonged to a neighbor.

He at first surveyed the ground with a watchful eye to see that no gardener was in sight; and he had glanced up at the windows of the mansion to assure himself that no one was looking; then he hurriedly helped himself to a bouquet and passed on.

To be sure, the garden was loaded with flowers, and those that he had gathered would never be missed. *Nevertheless, he had violated a principle; he had infringed upon the rights of others; he had taken property which did not belong to him.*

The only reproof administered by his mother when she learned of the fact was, "Oh, you shouldn't have done that." Then she put the flowers in a vase and set them on the center-table. It was a childish act, she said. The sort of thing that every boy does some time in his life. Yet the act was petty larceny; nothing more and nothing less. Similar thefts occur in every neighborhood where there are fruit-trees.

A man who has been most generous in the privileges he has granted neighbors, friends, and strangers in the use of the beautiful grounds surrounding his summer home planted a few cherry-trees some years ago, thinking it would be a pleasure to eat cherries from his own trees. So far he has been denied that privilege because his neighbors' children have helped themselves to the cherries before they were fairly ripe. They have not done this openly nor in the presence of the owner; they have sought occasions when they thought no one was looking, and they fled from the premises as soon as observed; yet their parents consider this mere "*childish mischief,*" and do not see that it calls for any serious consideration. But this is a species of vandalism and trains the mind of a child to wrong ideas regarding the rights of others.

The same child would probably be ashamed to enter his neighbor's house and steal cherries from the pantry shelf; but flowers and fruit growing on the property of a neighbor are just as much his own as though they had been plucked and carried indoors.

These fine distinctions of what constitutes honesty, refinement, and good breeding should be taught by every father and mother who desires children to become desirable citizens of the United States. They should become a part of the teaching of every public school. It is much more important that children should be impressed with these principles of high honesty and fine breeding than that they should be taught drawing, anatomy, or Latin. We will never have cleaner politics or fewer criminals and law-breakers in the land until we have more parents and more teachers who make it a business to impress upon the minds of little children the necessity to consider the rights of others in the small daily matters of life.

A peddler of cakes and condiments found his cart nearly empty. As he emerged from a house where he had been delivering packages a bevy of screaming youths, under fifteen years of age, ran out of reach, laughing at his look of consternation. They were children of respectable, church-going residents of the little suburban resort. It seemed to them an excellent jest to steal the man's cakes and cookies and feast upon them while his back was turned.

A child's mind should be formed to regard other people's property with respect before it reaches six years of age. This can be done by daily chats and pleasant conversation of the parents, fashioned to the understanding of the child. Little boys can be made to consider another boy's marbles and tin soldiers as personal property, not to be used or touched without the owner's permission and knowledge, and never to be marred or injured.

Little girls can be made to regard other children's dolls and toys in the same light. The impression should be indelibly fixed upon the delicate mind texture that any violation of this rule is vulgar and indicates lack of good breeding. Children so taught by tactful and considerate parents will never become thieves, and will never be guilty of petty purloinings of neighbors' flowers and fruits.

Day-schools and Sunday-schools may profitably employ a few moments three times each month at least to direct young minds to high, fine ideals in these small matters. It will save work and expense for courts of justice in years to come. And it will make the world a sweeter and more comfortable place for growing generations.

XIII

THE TOWER ROOM

And I have looked up through the veil of skies
When all the world was still and understood
That I am one with Nature and with God.

ARE you living up to the best there is in you? Are you even living up to one-half of that best?

Each one of us is a mansion. Each one of us is a mansion with its different stories, its ground floor, its upper rooms, and its tower. We must live many hours on the ground floor. We have our practical duties, our needs of the body, our daily cares which require our presence in the lower room.

Nearly all of us spend hours in the upper chambers, where we find repose and relaxation, but how many of us go every day into the tower room? How many of us, indeed, know, or, knowing, remember that we possess this tower room?

The ground-floor room is that mental condition which obliges us to think wholly of the needs of the body; the upper chambers are those moments or hours when we enjoy the pleasures and comforts of earth without anxiety or sordid cares; and the tower room is that exalted state of mind wherein we feel our close kinship to the Supreme Cause and to the Invisible Helpers of the universe.

Just a brief time spent in that room of your being each day will help you to peace, power, and prosperity. It will help you to grow in strength, health, usefulness, and happiness. If you have never entered this room you cannot reach it all at once. You will have to climb patiently to it. Many people belong to a church and believe in a creed and in heaven, yet have never entered the tower room in their own being.

Have you?

There are some things we know better to-day than any one knew a thousand or fifty years ago. Other things were known better a thousand and five thousand years ago than we know them.

Concentration was one of these things. The tendency of modern times is to scatter our mind forces—and to render us irritable, resentful, and ill-tempered. Here is a little formula which will help us all in our search for control, composure, and concentration. Sit in a quiet room, in a comfortable chair, erect, with the hands resting lightly on the knees.

Close the eyes, inhale a deep breath through the nostrils until counting seven, hold the breath while counting the same, and slowly exhale the same length of time. Think, as you do this, that you are taking in from God's universe good health, good will, success, happiness, and usefulness, and making them your own. Do this for five minutes only, morning and night, and see if your nerves do not come more under your control and the task of keeping amiable does not grow less difficult.

Of course you will not become *perfect* in a day, week, or year. You will have your ups and downs, your setbacks and your discouragements. But you will be helped and benefited by this simple exercise in a surprising degree.

Try it.

It is good for every human being on earth to breathe deeply and fill the whole body with pure, fresh air many times a day. It is good for every living thing to love and be loved. It is good for all human beings to live outdoors as much as possible and to stand and walk correctly.

There is no one so peculiarly constructed that he will not be benefited by these things; there is no one who will not be harmed by an opposite course; and there is no one who has a sorrow or a trouble so individual or special who will not be harmed by constant conversation about it or who will not be helped by the right attitude of mind toward this subject.

Science has proven that there is a physical change made in the brain-cells by each thought. Even a momentary sight of colors has produced an effect upon the color cells of an animal.

Imagine, then, what continual thought of any

kind must be doing for our own brains. Anger, revenge, fear, sorrow, despondency, worry, and melancholy are all little chisels chipping away at the physical structure of our heads, as well as changing the expressions of our faces, the attitudes of our bodies, and the chemicals of our mental atmosphere.

The woman who writes long, melancholy letters recounting the wrongs and troubles she has borne is shaping her brain to new sorrows and robbing herself of the power of concentration and of the vital force she needs to produce other and happier events. For events are greatly of our own molding, and many things which seem inevitable accidents are only the result of mental currents.

It is a curious thing how the body and mind react one on the other. If you sit before the mirror and frown for ten minutes you will begin to feel cross. If you sit and smile you will soon feel your heart growing merry. Train your body and your face to be alert, hopeful, and energetic, and luck will come to you ten times where it would come once to the despondent and drooping-visaged mortal.

I was told of a young girl who came to New York to find work and who had the most remarkable run of good fortune befall her. Her first effort was successful, and she left that position to fill another that offered twice the salary.

"Born to luck," a friend said to me.

Afterward I met the girl. She came on an errand. It was a day of rain and wind, but she blew into the room like a sunbeam and a summer breeze in one. She walked as if there were springs under her soles. She radiated light and cheer. She went directly to the object of her visit, made her errand known in a few concise, clearly spoken words, and went away, leaving me with the feeling that some vital part of the world's mechanism had passed before me. No wonder she is lucky, for her luck lies in herself.

If we are not born with it, let us cultivate it. We can.

And he who climbs daily to the Tower Room of his mind will surely one day sight the incoming Ship of Success, bearing to him in its hold all the highest and best dreams of his heart materialized.

XIV

LOVE

'Tis love, not creeds, that from a low condition
Leads mankind up to heights supreme and grand.
Oh, that the world could see and understand!

THE ideas of love between the sexes are changing with other conditions. According to one authority, romantic love between man and woman first came into the world with Dante's love for Beatrice. Before that period gallantry had existed; but only the gallantry of the male, who tries to attract the female—a purely sex impulse devoid of real romance and high sentiment.

In the Middle Ages and the days of the Christian Fathers woman was considered the author of all evil. She was even called "the door of hell." She was told she must live in continual penance on account of having brought sin into the world.

In the sixth century woman was forbidden to receive the Eucharist in the naked hand because of her impurity.

No Oriental religion ever reduced woman to

such degradation as did the fanaticism of these early Christian Fathers.

Here are some proverbs about women which men made popular in that era:

"Women and horses must be beaten."

"Women and money are the causes of all evils."

"Trust no woman even were she dead."

"If you are too happy, take a wife."

Montaigne recommended poetry to women because "it is a wanton, crafty art, disguised all for pleasure, all for show, just as they are."

John Stuart Mill once said in reference to those times:

"Some generations ago, when satires on women were in vogue, men thought it clever to insult women for being what men had made them."

The world has grown away from such ideas of women; and, with other changes, its viewpoint on what constitutes love has changed. Where once woman was supposed to be man's absolute chattel, she is now regarded as his comrade, mate, friend, and equal; and comradeship rather than service is demanded of her.

This question is propounded: "What is the highest form of woman's love for man?"

The question is at once simple and complex. Not every woman is endowed with the qualities which enable her to be a loveress. Not every woman so endowed meets the one capable of inspiring her. Not every woman who loves deeply possesses the spiritual and mental traits which alone render that love a blessing and a power for good to the recipient. There are women whose love blights and ruins. There are others whom to love or be loved by brings forth the latent powers in a man's nature and speeds him to the summits.

The highest form of love in a woman is that which ennobles not only the man who receives it, but her who gives it.

I have more than once seen a woman belittled and cheapened by a spaniel-like devotion to a man who was unworthy of the sentiment bestowed upon him and who was wearied by it. Such love is pitiful and holds no element of grandeur. It is merely one form of hysterics, and ought to come under the head of nervous diseases.

A great love, "the highest form of love," must contain a large element of womanly self-respect, and must dignify the giver as well as the recipient, even in its most extravagant phases.

It must to some degree absorb all other loves and make them secondary; yet if it renders the heart, which is its home, cruel to every living thing or blind to any duty, it ceases to be the "highest form of love."

Phædrus tells of a woman who loved her husband so much that in comparison father and mother seemed like strangers. This wife was Alcestis, the daughter of Pelius. She cheerfully laid down her life for her husband, and the gods accorded her the rare virtue of returning to earth when she felt like it.

It is quite possible that these parents deserved to seem like strangers to their daughter. Parental affection is not infrequently a most selfish sentiment, and one which in no sense includes the highest good for the children. To the majority of fathers and mothers the inner life of their offspring is as unknown as the Sanskrit language.

A mere tie of blood cannot force us to love what is unlovable.

If Alcestis passed from the home where the average domestic conditions exist into the full effulgence of a real love life, it is no wonder her parents seemed strangers to her. But if her newfound happiness caused her to ignore their feelings or to disregard a properly courteous and thoughtful code of conduct toward them, then it was not the "highest type of love."

To love truly, absorbingly, and passionately any one human being ought to make us more considerate and tender toward all humanity; just as the sunlight penetrates into dark recesses and warms and blesses every leaf and blade of grass, so a great love should cast its radiations upon all who come within its aura.

Our sympathies, our benevolence, our affections should all be deepened and widened by the presence of the great awakener in our hearts. A woman's faith in the man she loves should be firm and patient, yet it should not be blind.

It should expect results. It should not be satisfied to see him degenerate into selfishness, greediness, or immorality and make no protest or give no warning.

It should be a spur to his best nature, to his highest impulses.

Unless a man improves under the influence of a woman's love there is something wrong with her love or the man.

Every human being either improves or degenerates as years pass by. To the unprejudiced eye these subtle changes are visible year by year. There is no such thing as remaining stationary, mentally, morally, or physically.

A man may lose fortune and position, yet grow into a finer and more admirable manhood through the experience. He may gain wealth and at the same time lose or gain in moral worth, and these changes should be first visible to the eyes of the woman who loves him.

The highest type of love is not blind. It has the good of its object too near its heart to be blind to the changes which encompass it.

"Patient Griselda" was not a noble type of loving woman. She encouraged the brute and the tyrant in the man and allowed him to lower himself in the moral scale.

When a man says of a woman, "No matter what I do, she will say it is all right," be sure that woman is not giving the highest type of love. What a man ought to be able to say is: "No matter how appearances are against me, she will believe in me until I can explain to her, and if I make a mistake she will be the first to encourage me to begin anew and the quickest to forgive." No woman who loves utterly would think it a great sacrifice to give up her life for her lover were it necessary. Love is immortal and has no fear of death.

A perfect love must include spiritual sympathy, mental companionship, physical responsiveness. Any one of these elements lacking, love is crippled. Here is what Henry T. Finck has to say of Romantic love:

"Of all the rhetorical commonplaces in literature and conversation none is more frequently repeated than the assertion that love as depicted in a thousand novels and poems every year has existed at all times and in every country, immutable as the mountains and the stars, but romantic love is a modern sentiment less than a thousand years old.

"Not till Dante's *Vita Nuova* appeared was the gospel of modern love—the romantic adoration of a maiden by a youth—revealed for the first time in definite language. Genius, however, is always in advance of its age, in emotions as well as in thoughts, and the feelings experienced by Dante were obviously not shared by his contemporaries, who found them too subtle and sublimated for their comprehension. And, in fact, they were too ethereal to quite correspond with reality. The strings of Dante's lyre were strung too high and, touched by his magic hand, gave forth harmonic overtones too celestial for mundane ears to hear."—*Romantic Love and Personal Beauty*.

This curious and interesting book, which deals with all phases and attributes of love, has nothing whatever to say of Platonic love.

There is wholesome, sincere friendship between man and woman. It is in no sense Platonic love. The moment we use the word love we speak of a claim, a necessity. The element of love entering into our affection, we find the object necessary to our happiness.

When a man becomes in any way necessary to a woman, or a woman to a man, the tie is no longer mere "friendship," nor can any trumped-up makeshift of "Platonism" disguise its real nature. When any human being becomes a part of your plans for pleasure or happiness each day or each week or each month, there is danger ahead for you if that being is of the opposite sex and not related to you by blood ties.

Wreathe it over as you will with flowery talk of Platonic love, nevertheless you are marching to the chasm of dangerous experiment. You may as well carry a lighted match into a dynamite factory and say you are safe. A man's housekeeper or secretary may be necessary to his comfort or to the successful accomplishment of his business. He may say, "I could not get along without her." But that is another question.

It is when the social and holiday side of the

man's nature feels the necessity of some one woman to share his enjoyment that he needs to be on his guard if he wishes to avoid giving or receiving pain or finding himself in some sort of trouble.

It has been said: "There are two great problems of life—the problem of sex and the problem of God. It is hard to say which is the more tormenting; it is enough that each is a whirling maelstrom."

But in the problem of God we can always fall back on the consciousness that *Love* and progress cover the whole question, while in the problem of sex, love is only the higher phase, and before we climb to it we are in danger of stumbling into the mire below if we are not eternally on guard.

XV

THOUGHT-NAILS

> Though desolate
> The way may seem, command thy fate,
> Send forth thy thought, achieve, achieve!

RISE above fear. Do not be a slave to the fear of poverty, the fear of sickness, the fear of sudden disaster or death. Though the earth may quake, and the floods rise, and the cyclone blow, and the lightnings glare, and the flames rage, let your spirit keep its calm. It is eternal, and nothing can harm it.

Do not spoil days of peace and serenity and comfort by continual fear of things which may never happen; for if they do happen the energy of your mind will be needed to meet and conquer them. Fear is a rat in the wall, undermining energy and courage and strength.

Were you to see a carpenter with a barrel of nails building a house, and if you knew he could have only that one barrel of nails, and that the house must be completed at a certain period of time, would you not think the man a fool if you saw him throwing the nails one by one into the sand or the ocean or the flames? Every thought we send out is a nail in the construction of Character, that mansion we are sent to this earth-plane to build. To use these thought-nails in fear, worry, despondency, gloom, hatred, resentment, and doubt of God and ourselves is as foolish and wicked as would be the waste of nails by the carpenter who had contracted to build the house made by hands.

Never before in the last century had America such need of knowledge of the power of the mind to control circumstances as *now*. Never was there a greater demand for the exercise of *self-control* and self-assertion. There was never a time when those who believe in prophecies had greater need of balance and common sense mixed with this belief. There is no question but many people possess the *sixth sense* which enables them to see some approaching events. But few, very few, possess the knowledge of the *time* such events will transpire.

Therefore it is unwise to be one of those "who, through fear of death, live always in bondage," and who by continual fear of calamity bring it nearer.

There is an invisible world about us in which events which occur here are formulated; and there are eyes on earth which see those events in the process. In centuries to come all human beings will possess this sixth sense. But not all who pretend to possess it are to be trusted. And however true may be the prophet who foretells your future at the time of the telling, remember *you are a part of destiny, and you can modify events and turn disasters into blessings by your mental attitude.*

This you cannot do if your mind is full of fear.

Fear is a devil of man's own making; have nothing to do with him and he will leave you. Entertain him and he will destroy you.

However scientific may be the causes on which some prophet bases his assertion that a great disaster hangs over your locality or yourself, begin each day with an assertion of *trust in the Creator of all things.* Then clear your mind of all despondency, all hate, and all revenge. Forgive everybody who has wronged you and saturate your heart with the thought, "I am surrounded by a circle of Divine Love, and nothing but good can come to me."

If you find fear and gloom approaching the citadel of your mind during the day, say: "I was placed on earth to make the most of my opportunities. I am here for a good purpose, or I would not be here. Whatever occurs, it is my part to be calm, trustful, and helpful." When you hear people talking of flood and earthquake and war and pestilence, fill your mind with sunshine, serenity, peace, and health.

If you do this persistently and systematically you will, in the event that any of these disasters come, find yourself a rock of safety for others, and you will be protected by seemingly miraculous circumstances in the midst of peril.

Most of us shelter some pet fear in our hearts. Many of us give room, rent free, to a whole brood of fears. The old orthodox religion of our early Christian Fathers was built on fear. The Puritans loved the fear of God more than they loved the love of God or humanity.

A more wholesome creed is taught in our day; even the churches are beginning to teach love in place of fear.

The New Thought philosophy makes fear the only devil. Yet even those who know the foolishness and danger of entertaining fear find it difficult to exile the demon from their hearts and minds so absolutely that it cannot find some window left open through which it may creep in and curl up in one corner.

The fear of poverty, when it becomes a settled thought, is classed as insanity by brain specialists. Many men of wealth die in misery, victims of this mania. Fear of being slighted or injured by others, when indulged and dwelt upon, becomes another form of insanity called paranœa. Fear of misfortune and bad luck caused a successful and healthy man to commit suicide recently because he found the ship on which he had taken passage for Europe was to sail on the thirteenth of the month. So deeply rooted had become his superstitious fear of the date that he lost his reason.

Fear of death caused a man who was challenged to a duel to kill himself before the hour set for the duel arrived. Fear of sickness sends many a man and woman to the sanitarium and many others to the grave.

Yet how to rid our minds of these fears, or others like them, is ofttimes a serious problem. The mind that has long entertained fear becomes weakened, and is seemingly unable, alone and unassisted, to drive out the enemy to peace and happiness.

Then is the time when an appeal to the Higher Forces, to the "Invisible Helpers," will bring its sure response.

Go alone to your best-loved room, or to any spot where you can be sure of silence and seclusion. Sit quietly and breathe deeply, until your nerves are calmed; then lift your whole nature in an earnest appeal to the "Great Friends," the "Invisible Helpers," to come to your aid. Ask them to take away fear from your heart and to replace it with infinite trust, absolute faith, joy unspeakable.

After you have made this appeal, assert that peace, happiness, and trust are yours. Say to your subjective mind, when you are falling asleep, "I am taking my thinking, objective mind to the land of sleep; I leave you in charge. Fill my being with serenity, confidence in God, and in myself, drive away fear and despondency."

Then make your little assertion the very last conscious moment, "I am encircled by the arms of Divine Love, and nothing but good can come to me."

You will waken with a new sense of security and strength in the morning. If during the day old fear tries to creep in, make your good-night assertion again and refuse to think of fear-inspiring things. Recall to yourself the innumerable times when fears which you have entertained in the past proved to be nothing but the result of your own imagination.

If you are inclined to question the existence of Angel Helpers, or Invisible Friends, rest on the fact that there can be produced a mighty army of brilliant and sane souls who have proven these things to their own satisfaction; and that the greatest achievements in the history of the world have been accomplished by men and women who believed in Spiritual Intelligences and their power to aid mankind.

These intelligences, these helpers, do *exist;* and they *will* bring you into the kingdom of your own soul and drive away fear if you ask their assistance. But after it is given, and while you are asking, you must help yourself by practical and persistent methods. Their work is to help those who help themselves; not to do your work for you.

Peace, Power, and Plenty belong to you. Claim your own.

XVI

A MENTAL INVENTORY

When life gives
The burden of a duty, difficult
And hard to carry, then rejoice, O Soul,
And know thyself one chosen for high things.

WHAT have you accomplished this year?

I mean, what have you accomplished *that will last?*

You may have made money, or gained a social foothold, or created a rôle in the dramatic world, or written a book or play or opera; you may have traveled and received adulation from foreign lands, but that is not what I mean.

Not one of these things will last. They all pass away with time. Money, fame, beauty, power, all pass away.

Character only remains. What have you done toward building your character?

Sit down alone by yourself in a quiet room and turn the lights low and think it over.

Have you grown stronger in any worthy principle? Have you exercised self-control in your appetites? Is it easier or harder for you to resist taking "a drink" when you know it is not good for you; or to decline food that you are conscious disagrees with you and leaves unpleasant effects afterward?

It is *either* easier or more difficult; we never stand still. You are certainly a bit stronger or a bit weaker in your will power than you were a year ago to-day.

Which is it?

Have you gained anything intellectually in this year? Do you know more in any desirable line of study or research? Or has your brain been frittered away on the daily news and light fiction, and things which have done you no good more than to pass away time? Have you stored up one historical fact or scientific piece of information that will help you, or have you thought seriously on any topic which developed your brain powers? Have you made any progress in any art, profession, or accomplishment?

Have you cultivated self-denial for the sake of others; have you restrained yourself in selfish pleasures and habits now and then, that you might give more time and pleasure to some one near you—a parent, a child, a husband, a wife?

Have you thought a little about the life to come? The years are hurrying by; ahead lies the path that we must all take alone one of these days. Have you given a little thought to where that path leads?

There is nothing of material possessions or

achievements you can take with you. Only the worth-while pleasures and the unselfish deeds and the best thoughts can accompany us on that last journey.

Have you tried to inform your mind on the part your thoughts play in building your body here, and your place and plane in the life after? It is an interesting study and will pay you for the time you give to it.

Have you grown stronger or weaker physically this last year? If weaker, what is the cause? Not hard work; for work harms no man if he lives, breathes, thinks, and eats properly. If you are weaker you have violated some common-sense law. You have failed to use all your lung-cells every day; you have overloaded your system with food which did it no good; and you have worried and been despondent. Any and all these things break down the health. But whatever you have failed to do this year can be done next year. Only we must first be conscious of our failures before we can remedy them.

So take your hour alone to-day and think it all over. Balance up your books and start right to-morrow. Every day begins a new year.

Many a man will no doubt reckon his success in business as the only achievement necessary to jot down in his ledger. He has made money; he has enabled his wife to dress well; he has sent his children to fashionable schools; he has a new motor-car, or several new motors, and feels that his year is a great triumph.

Some woman may be quite satisfied with having made sacrifices for her children; she has toiled for them; she has dressed plainly that they might dress well; and she has been in every possible way a help to her husband in the economical method of using his income for the best interests of the family.

But what, dear sir or madam, has been your daily deportment in your home or in your business? Your money is not the important thing to consider at this time of year. It is your character. What progress have you made in the last year toward developing an admirable and lovable disposition? What sort of memories are you storing up for those nearest to you—wife, husband, children, or business associates?

They may outlive you, and how will they remember you?

Are you doing by them exactly as you would like to be done by? That is not a new idea, but it is quite as well worth your consideration as if it were. You may be a busy man, weighed down with matters of political or business importance, and you will think my question a trivial one, perhaps. *But nothing on earth is of more importance than doing right by our daily associates.* Nothing here or hereafter can atone for our neglect to bring out the *best* in those nearest us.

If you are cold, irritable, indifferent, nagging,

selfish, stingy, or thoughtless in your home or your office or shop, you are bringing out the worst —not the best — qualities in others. You are spoiling beautiful days, weeks, and months for others, and that is more criminal than spoiling their property; the time-despoiler, the happiness-slayer is the most cruel vandal on earth.

Besides wronging others, you are ruining yourself in the recollection of those who outlive you.

If you are devoting your whole time and strength to making money for your wife and children, or if you, as their mother, are sacrificing pleasure and youth to give them advantages, do not imagine you are doing all that is required of you. To be agreeable, to be patient, to be companionable — those are the qualities which help to make life worth living for those near us. It is a tragedy to spoil one day for another human being by a lack of these qualities, even though we bestow a fortune upon that being when we pass on.

It is a tragedy to be remembered as an uncomfortable and unamiable person, even of large virtues.

How do you imagine those about you will remember you when you are gone?

XVII

THE SMALL TOWN

Along this world benighted
  Where clouds and shadows roll,
One narrow path is lighted
  For each immortal soul.
The path of Love's endeavor
  To show the God within,
And who walks there will never
  Be slave of fear or sin.

DO not let your minds narrow down to the limits of your town; do not let your ideas become dwarfed, your ambitions stunted, your outlook limited. There is no need of it in this day and age of low-priced literature and free libraries.

You can keep in mental touch with the whole world if you wish to do it. There is no need of confining your information to the social column of your country paper. Read the magazines and weeklies and book reviews when you cannot obtain the books. Think of yourself as an important factor in the *world*—not merely of your town or church. Try and be broad and large in your outlook.

The moment you find yourself dwelling on

thoughts of neighborhood gossip and petty scanals turn your back on your lesser self and search for your real self—the noble, great-hearted being you were destined to be. Read history and meditate upon the lives of great men and women. When you are about to pass Mary Jones by without speaking to her because you heard some one had suspected her of questionable conduct, stop and think of Joan of Arc, Mme. Roland, Father Damien, Nathan Hale, Abraham Lincoln, or a hundred other colossal figures you can call to mind. They will scare away all petty prejudices and make you ashamed of yourself. Think of our Pilgrim fathers and mothers and all the wonderful strength of character it required to live their lives in those dangerous and difficult times. It will make your own cares and troubles seem trivial. Avoid judging humanity from the standards set up in your town. Be liberal, and remember that climate and environment have much to do with people's ideas of behavior. Try and cultivate a loving interest in your associates.

It is a strange fact that in small towns so little affection or love exists among the inhabitants. One would think it sure to be found in the quiet country hamlets, where the few people are dependent upon one another for enjoyment. But instead we find jealousy, criticism, and indifference prevailing in such places. I have lived in the lonely country farming town, in the small hamlet, and in the crowded cities, and I must confess that it is in the latter I have found greater and more spontaneous affection and readier sympathy among people, together with broader judgments. In the average country hamlet one needs to be ill or an object of charity to bring out the tenderness in the hearts of his neighbors. Let it be known that sickness or poverty has visited a household, and the tongue of gossip is silenced and the indifferent or disagreeable air gives place to solicitous kindness — while the trouble lasts! But, remember, we cannot all in this world be invalids or beggars. Yet we all love sympathy and companionship and appreciation.

Many women in the country love to play Lady Bountiful merely for the gratification of being looked up to. But a greater nature finds pleasure in showing affectionate interest in an equal on whom it can bestow nothing but friendship. Think every day how large the world is compared to your town, yet do not despise your town in consequence. Respect it as part of the great Consolidated Company of Human Beings, and make it as interesting a place as possible by your own mental, moral, and social qualities.

Study, think, read, work, and *love*. Sympathize with your neighbors' aims, ambitions, efforts, hopes, and trials. Cheer them all you can, and never allow a thought of jealousy or envy to enter your mind if some one seems to you to be succeeding better than you or yours.

Do not permit yourself to be small and petty because you live in a small town. Be so large of soul that you will dignify the town in the mind of any one who knows it is your place of residence.

XVIII

WHAT IS "CHARM"?

Oh, a great world, a fair world, a true world I find it:
  A sun that never forgets to rise,
  On the darkest night a star in the skies,
And a God of love behind it.

THE French women confess that the American women are handsome, well dressed, entertaining, and brilliant, but this is their criticism: "The American woman has no charm."

It was an American woman who told me of hearing this remark made many times in Paris.

"Now, what do they mean by charm?" she asked.

You might as well ask what is meant by saying a flower has no perfume. *Charm*, in a woman, is as subtle a thing as perfume in a flower. It does not pertain to personal appearance; it does not pertain to accomplishments; it does not pertain to manner, education, dress, or conversation, *yet it permeates all these*. And without it all of these are rendered meaningless.

A woman may be fascinating without being charming. She may fascinate with smiles and coquetries, which we know are insincere, but which nevertheless hold us in a spell. The charming woman is almost always an unselfish woman. She forgets herself when she is in the presence of others, or shall I say that she *remembers herself and her duty to be agreeable.* Perhaps it is this higher consciousness of self—the better self—which makes a large portion of charm of manner.

The charming woman never allows the conversation to dwell long upon herself, and she never monopolizes the conversation. She leads others to talk, and is interested in what others say and do. She is always tactful. She avoids the topics that are distasteful to others and introduces those which will be agreeable. The charming woman usually possesses a certain amount of feminine vanity: she likes to please, not only to please the mind and the heart, but the eye.

She usually dresses becomingly and takes excellent care of her person, so that she exhales an atmosphere of beauty, even if she possesses no absolute beauty of face or form.

The woman famed for her beauty is rarely charming, because she has been so spoiled and flattered from the cradle up that her heart is almost always devoid of the sympathy which must form a strong part of charm. When a beautiful woman is unselfish and sympathetic and loving, her charm usually becomes historic.

It was said that Madame Récamier was as

beloved by her own sex as she was admired by the opposite. She was goodness and charm personified, as well as beauty. A woman friend said of her once: "First of all she is good; then she is brilliant; then she is beautiful."

Ninon de L'Enclos, who was not "good" like Récamier, was charming. In spite of her free and easy morals, she left the impression of great charm upon the world. Her moral derelictions are forgotten in her charm. She was kindness itself to other women, and to the age of eighty-four retained her hold upon the affections of both sexes.

Charm must spring from an affectionate nature and from a heart which desires to give pleasure rather than to be admired. But the charming woman usually receives more admiration than the professional beauty, the great genius, or the most brilliant of her sex who do not possess charm. Of all compliments a woman can receive, the greatest is to be called "charming" when "goodness" is added.

XIX

KEEP STILL

Would you believe in Presences Unseen—
In life beyond this earthly life?
Be still;
Be stiller yet; and listen.

WHAT is your morning conversation? Are you telling each member of the family how poorly you slept, what nightmares disturbed you, how wakeful you were, and what a temperature you have?

Are you disturbing the peace and comfort of those about you with talk of nerves and headaches?

Then you are committing a sin against God and humanity. You are defiling the atmosphere with mental emanations of disease and nervousness and creating discord for yourself and others. I have seen a whole family's happiness for the day destroyed by one hysterical woman who insisted on having every one feel her pulse and note its rapid beat, while she recounted all the causes which had led to her delicate nervous condition.

Meantime she was devoutly religious and believed it was God's will she should suffer. But was it "God's will" she should make every one in her vicinity suffer? God has nothing to do with suffering and disease. He never made it. He made Love, Health, opportunities for happiness. In each soul He put His own divine qualities, Love, the Creative instincts—will power and the ability to be, to do, to know.

Men have perverted—misused, or left unused—these qualities and substituted hate, lust, self-indulgence, ignorance, and indolence—and as a result disease and poverty and unhappiness are in the world. They are *not* God's will. You are not a Christian or a religious woman if you are talking about your diseases to every one about you.

You may be born with a tendency to disease through the many wrong thoughts and habits of ancestors. But if you fill your soul full of Love—great, deep, high, broad, profound Love—and if you live with a prayer of thankfulness in your heart to God for Life, and believe health is your right and that it will be given to you, and fashion your whole conduct to suit that thought, *it will be given.*

It will never come if you harp on the old strain of "God's will" when you suffer and persist in having an audience for every pain. Not only will it never come to you, but you will destroy the health of those about you. You pride yourself on being a good woman and a heroine where sickness is concerned. All invalids do. But you are not a good woman if you spoil the beautiful morning hours by a recital of your symptoms and send out into other minds microbes of diseased thought. It is not that we must never mention our indisposition. Rigid rules in any direction do more harm than good. A silent martyr usually makes people uncomfortable with the eloquence of silence.

If you break your limb, say so, and say it will heal. If you break any law of health and fall ill, confess it. To "deny" it is ridiculous, and creates only ridicule and antagonism. But, while you confess it, affirm your speedy restoration. If you have not been able to keep yourself from serious illness by right thoughts and methods of life, employ wise skill to restore you. But for God's sake, humanity's sake, and your own sake, stop this eternal harping on your diseases.

Stop describing your symptoms, all the awful "operations" you have passed through, and let your relatives and friends take a respite from feeling your pulse, finding your temperature, and looking at your tongue.

Keep still and be well.

XX

"THE DANGEROUS AGE"

God finished woman in the twilight hour,
And said, "To-morrow thou shalt find thy place:
Man's complement, the mother of the race,
With love the motive power—
The one compelling power."

A VERY young married woman ought to cast a thoughtful glance along the future and make some provision for middle age. Not provision for a rainy day, but preparation which will insure a sunny season when middle life arrives. At twenty-five, forty seems far away; but that age speeds toward us with the velocity of a flying express train.

It is a beautiful age when we meet it with the right understanding of all it may mean and with wise preparation. Culture, accomplishments, a perfectly developed body, a well-trained mind, an enlightened spirit, a sympathetic heart, an uplifted soul—all these mean a lovely middle and old age. And all these things must, to reach their best development, be begun in the earlier season of life.

Between the ages of thirty-five and fifty-five the life of the average woman becomes either gray or gay.

In the world of fashion the "gay" matron is to be found. She leads in her circle, she invents new amusements, she delights in being called "dangerous," and she practises all the arts of coquetry upon the men she meets, especially men younger than herself. Life is a feverish dream to her, and she is never happy save when in the midst of social excitement. Not infrequently she brings a scandal upon her name through indiscretions of conduct, and she figures more frequently in the divorce court than do younger women.

In the quieter walks of life the women who reach thirty-five begin to find the world assuming a gray color. All the gold and crimson fades; the ambitions of early youth are lost, with many of its illusions; romance has faded, and duty only remains. They perform the tasks required of them as wives and mothers in a mechanical manner, and become "settled" in figure and stolid in face and prematurely old in appearance. Yet at thirty-five a woman is entering the very best period of her whole life.

From then until sixty at least she should be in possession of her most ripened mental powers, and she should be most pleasing to the eye, like a radiant autumn landscape. Life should be a thing of delight to her, and she ought to enjoy it with more intensity than ever before because of her deeper understanding and broader sympathies and clearer judgment.

It is not difficult for a student of human nature to understand how the society woman of middle age becomes "gay." Woman's emotional nature is at its height at thirty-five and forty, and she craves love more than in her shy and unformed youth. Mrs. Grundy incites her votaries to folly and shuts her eyes to indiscretions so long as they are not flagrant. If marriage has proven a disappointment to the society woman she easily plunges into the vortex of fashionable dissipation and finds her only enjoyment in its whirlpool of folly.

The very craving for sentiment in the heart of the mature woman in the village or country town is what makes life assume a gray color for her. She is ashamed of her own weakness and puts away the thoughts which assail her as evidences of a morbid mind. She tells herself that she is no longer young, that she has outlived her romantic period, and that she must be satisfied to accept the dull old age which lies before her. So she meets it half-way upon the road to show she does not care.

The husband of such a woman does not dream what is going on in her mind and soul. He has become a money-maniac or is absorbed in politics or in the pursuit of some career. If his home is well ordered, his wife and children comfortable, it is as far as his ambitions lead him.

He regards sentiment as a thing of the past, and it never occurs to him to pay his wife a compliment or speak a word of love to her. That would savor of weakness to his mind. So the gray years go by, and if one day he notices that his wife looks very old and commonplace he feels a sense of personal injury in the fact and wonders why some women lose their charm so much sooner than others.

The face cannot stay young unless the heart is kept warm. Every woman who passes thirty ought to keep her brain, heart, and mind alive and warm with human sympathy and emotion. She ought to interest herself in the lives of others and to make her friendship valuable to the young.

She should keep her body supple and avoid losing the lines of grace, and she should select some study or work to occupy spare hours and to lend a zest to the coming years. Every woman in the comfortable walks of life can find time for such a study. No woman of tact, charm, refinement, and feeling need ever let her husband, (unless she has married a clod,) become indifferent or commonplace in his treatment of her. Man reflects to an astonishing degree womans' sentiments for him.

Keep sentiment alive in your own heart, madam, and in the heart of your husband. If he sees that other men admire you he will be more alert to the necessity of remaining your lover.

Take the happy, safe, medium path between a gray and a gay life by keeping it radiant and bright. Read and think and talk of cheerful, hopeful, interesting subjects. Avoid small gossip, and be careful in your criticism of neighbors. Sometimes we must criticize, but speak to people whose faults you feel a word of counsel may amend—not of them to others.

Make your life after it reaches its noon glorious with sunlight, rich with harvests, and bright with color. Be alive in mind, heart and body. Be joyous without giddiness, loving without silliness, attractive without being flirtatious, attentive to others' needs without being officious, and instructive without too great a display of erudition.

Be a noble, loving, lovable woman.

XXI

THE SENSE OF HUMOR

Out of the blackness groping
  My heart finds a world in bloom;
For it somehow is fashioned for hoping
  And it cannot live in the gloom.

IT is a great thing to possess a sense of humor. It is a misfortune to be devoid of that sense.

To be able to see the "funny" side of life enables one to laugh where others cry and to be amused where others are angry and distressed over unexpected or undesired events.

The man with a sense of humor loses his way on a journey and wanders far afield, but he is so amused over his queer experience that he keeps himself from being nervous or out of temper.

The woman who has an acute sense of the ridiculous or the comical is able to laugh when left without servants just as she is expecting a houseful of guests; and she receives her guests in such excellent spirits that they all join in her mirth, and in some way the difficult situation is sure to resolve itself into a huge joke, and everybody has the best kind of a time.

The woman devoid of humor in that situation develops nervous prostration. Women are said by scientists to lack a sense of humor. The German nation, like the English, is supposed to be quite devoid of the quality of brain which enables a human being to find easily something laughable in life. But quite recently a lady living in Berlin proved the exception to the rule, if rule it be. When she learned that two aeronauts had dropped, with their basket, from a balloon right through the roof of her house and into her boudoir, destroying chimney, roof, and bric-à-brac as they went down, she sent the gentlemen a note expressing her regret that she was "not at home" when they dropped in.

Many another woman would have gone into hysterics and then appealed to the courts to award her damages.

An American woman had planned a week of amusement and pleasure at the house party of a friend. It was to be the star week of the year. But when it arrived she was lying in bed with a broken limb, caused by jumping from a window to escape fire. When her friend and expected hostess called to condole with her she found the patient jeopardizing the splintered limb by her laughter. "It strikes me as very droll," said the invalid, "that a fire and a broken leg constitute my pleasure this star week of the year."

Yet there is another side to this quality of humor in men and women. When we laugh at ourselves, at our own foibles and follies, at fate and circumstance, it is all very well.

But when we laugh at other people—not *with them*, but *at them*—when we make them targets for fun and ridicule, the keen sense of humor with which we excuse ourselves hardly changes the fact that we are not kind, cultured, or loyal to our friends or fellow-men.

A sweet-natured woman gave a reception for a celebrity. The celebrity attended it, but spent the entire evening in sly and covert ridicule of the hostess and the friends she had invited to meet the guest of honor.

She excused herself afterward to an acquaintance on the ground that she was possessed of "a keen sense of humor," and that the hostess and her friends were really a very droll lot.

Still another woman, afflicted with the same excess of humor in her make-up, ridiculed a simple little entertainment given by home talent at the house of a friend. The hostess had no idea of giving a Wagnerian performance, but the attitude of the lady of humorous proclivities was that of one who had bought the privilege of a First-Nighter to criticize an ambitious opening, not the attitude of a kind and cultured woman in the home of a friend. The human mind is a sort of trap, and it catches whatever we set it to obtain.

Everywhere about us are funny things, ridiculous things, sad, glad, and bad things, happening; and there are sweet things, and beautiful things, and hopeful things, and merry and dramatic occurrences.

We will catch and retain in our mental traps those things which we seek. To seek the humorous and amusing side of life is an excellent habit; but to become a chronic "guyer," and to ridicule where we could at least remain silent or where we could bestow a kindly word of appreciation for the *motive*, places us on the level with the circus clown.

Much of this ridicule and guying indulged in by human beings comes, not from a keen sense of humor, but from petty, despicable jealousy. In country towns there is always some one girl who makes a practice of ridiculing the admirers of other young women. But the habit cannot be attributed to an unusual appreciation of the comical, however much she may claim it to be. It is merely the outcome of envy. Before you laugh at other people, their manners, habits, or performances, be sure you know *why* you laugh. To laugh at the wrong time or thing is often an evidence of ignorance and vulgarity.

Two bell-boys at a hotel watched the painful progress of a partially paralyzed young man across the office and nudged each other and laughed audibly.

The cruelty of these boys was the result of ignorance. Their mothers had never taught them to feel sympathy and show courtesy to the afflicted.

Whatever they saw that was unusual they considered "funny." A great many grown people who have had opportunities for culture are equally vulgar when it comes to the delicate sensibilities of their fellow-pilgrims.

There are a few rules which a mother might teach her children as soon as they arrive at a thinking age regarding the laughable things of life.

Never laugh at the crippled, the deformed, the old, the poor, the badly dressed, or the unfortunate human being.

Never laugh at the pygmy or giant, unless they are performing in public where they *expect* laughter.

Never laugh at the foreigner who wears a different costume from the one you are accustomed to see. Remember, your costume would look as strange in his country, and in all probability not nearly so artistic.

When you are a guest never laugh at the entertainment which is offered you unless you are convinced it was intended to make you laugh. Just as you would refrain from criticising the food at table, even if it did not appeal to your palate, refrain from criticising the entertainment your friends offer you.

Laugh to keep yourself and the world about you in good humor. Never laugh to make others uncomfortable.

XXII

SCIENCE AND THE AURA

> Science, the doubter of accepted truths,
> Shall yet reveal God's secrets to the world
> And prove the facts it seeks to overthrow.

IN the oldest religions of the earth we find mention of the auras.

Auras and haloes are generally supposed to be crowns of light hovering over the heads of saints.

By practical-minded people the aura has long been regarded as a delusion of overwrought sensibilities.

Religious devotees, mediums, fanatics, poets, and insane beings were alone considered susceptible to these hallucinations.

Theosophists have always talked of auras as a part of the mental and physical belongings of every human being.

But by the material mind the theosophist is considered insane. And now comes Science, lagging along, with its proof of what the theosophists and other advanced souls have long known to be true.

That there is a haze or atmosphere surrounding

the human body and differing in the case of each individual, and that its existence is susceptible of physical proof, is the assertion made by Dr. Walter J. Kilner, a London physician, whose investigation of the subject has covered many years.

In a book Dr. Kilner gives the result of his investigations and invites those interested in the subject to make the same experiments, using the means which he employed to aid the eye in perceiving what he calls the human aura.

Dr. Kilner maintains that he has not only perceived what the clairvoyants have declared they saw, but even more. Not only do people possess auras, according to Dr. Kilner, but their auras, differing in the case of each individual, and very distinctly so in the case of women and men, are probably inherited, he thinks. Then, too, he says the physical condition affects at once the aura.

Whatever value the revelation of auras will have for the scientific world, Dr. Kilner thinks will lie in this point, for, being thus affected by physical conditions, auras will be a distinct aid in diagnosis.

Dr. Kilner gives examples in his book of persons suffering from epilepsy whose auras all exhibited a different outline from those of persons in good health. The healthier a person the more distinct his aura.

"The influence of heredity and temperament upon the aura," says the doctor, "is one of the most fascinating parts of this subject, and at the same time it does not require a prophet to foresee that an inquirer in this direction is likely to reap a big harvest."

Dr. Kilner likens the aura to the rays proceeding from a magnet. When looked at through his screen the magnetic cloud emanating from a magnet appeared distinctly visible in the same manner as did the human aura. He believes that the forces giving rise to the human aura are quite distinct from those producing the magnetic cloud, and that there is more than a single force at work, one producing the outer and another the inner aura.

These forces, he believes, are most probably generated in the body in some such way as the nervous force.

He also lays down the law that the aura is influenced by the will power. He has made many experiments which have gone to prove this, such as telling a person to will that a ray should extend from his finger toward another person. The ray, he says, soon made its appearance and disappeared directly the patient left off willing.

Dr. Kilner mentions a young woman twenty years old upon whom he experimented, and whom he asked to shoot rays from her two shoulders, first one and then the other. The beams manifested themselves almost directly, taking an upward and outward direction. She was asked to turn sideways then, and to will a ray to extend from the tip of her nose.

"In this," said the doctor, "she was perfectly successful, as it appeared almost immediately and stretched outward seven or eight inches. This was beyond the external margin of the visible outer aura."

Dr. Kilner lays distinct emphasis on the statement that he is not an occultist, nor does he make pretense to clairvoyancy. What he wants people to understand is that his researches have been entirely physical and that they can be repeated by any one.

"There cannot be the slightest doubt," he says, "as to the reality of the existence of an aura enveloping human beings, and this will be in a short time a universally accepted fact, now that it can be made visible to any one possessing normal eyesight. It would indeed be strange if the aura did not vary under different circumstances, and we firmly believe that a study of its modifications will show that they will have a diagnostic value."

Now, in the face of these scientific facts, it behooves each one of us to give some thought to the subject of auras.

We need to realise, first of all, that the aura is as much a part of us as our heads or hands. And that its shape and color are largely under our control.

Long ago the theosophists and clairvoyants said the dark-gray or green or muddy-brown aura was an evidence of unwholesome conditions of mind and body. Blue and pink and yellow were desirable shades for auras, indicating spirituality, affection, and intellect.

Dr. Kilner's book classifies people according to the color of their auras—those whose auras appeared to be blue, blue mixed with gray, and those with gray auras. Taking these classifications, he examined one hundred persons. He found forty in the blue-aura class. Of these forty persons none was below the average in mental power, and some were distinctly above it.

Thirty-six were in the second class, with auras showing a combination of blue and gray. Among these were two epileptics and one with meningitis. Seventeen had gray auras, and among these seventeen were two eccentric people, six epileptics, one insane person, and three who were mentally dull.

From those observations the doctor deduces the theory that if you have a blue aura you are most apt to be mentally fit, but if your aura is gray you are probably a bit deficient in intellectual power.

Now that science so closely agrees with the seers, we cannot reasonably doubt that psychic people have seen and do see auras. And it renders one a bit uncomfortable to think how many clear-seeing eyes may have beheld very ugly auras emanating from us.

Every thought, emotion, and feeling is having its influence in shaping and coloring our auras.

If we were given free choice of selecting a hideous or a beautiful head-dress, or hat, there would be no hesitation about the one chosen.

We are given this privilege of selecting our auras.

Or at least we are given the privilege and power to change those which may have been given us by inheritance from other lives or which may have been created by wrong methods of education in this life.

Not only is your aura visible to many clear-seeing eyes and to the eye of Science, but its influence is felt by every one.

The dark-gray or brown aura sends out a gloomy and depressing influence; and the light, bright colors send out love and cheer and aspiration to all who come in your presence.

And as you color and beautify this aura you are helping build your body into greater strength and your brain into greater power.

Think of the aura as an absolute possession, belonging to you, and given you to make beautiful in its appearance and its influence; and so surely as you work toward this result shall peace and prosperity and health come to you and your power for usefulness increase.

XXIII

THE MONEY QUESTION

And man shall leave his fevered dreams behind him—
  The dreams of avarice and lust and sin;
And seek his Lord; yea, he shall seek and find Him
  In his own soul, where He has always been.

WE talk much of woman's independence in America, of the generosity and unselfishness of American husbands, and of the wonderful privileges enjoyed by wives in all classes of society in this land of the free and home of the brave. But there is another side to the picture, not frequently shown to the public.

In every city and town in America, even to a certain degree in our largest metropolis (and second and third largest), exist women who dress well, live well, and donate generous sums to charity, yet *who never have the handling of one dollar without asking for it and without saying to what purpose it is to be dedicated.*

These women are the wives of well-to-do men; many of them are the wives of men of large wealth; and such a condition is reputed to exist in the home of one of America's most widely known multimillionaires.

Knowledge of the humiliating position of these wives comes to the public through the secretive methods by which they endeavor to possess themselves of a few dollars of their husband's money without having to submit to his catechism. One woman asked her French teacher to make a bill of double size, and when he cashed the check to give her the amount remaining after his bill was paid. Another follows a similar course with a dressmaker; another with a physician or dentist.

In every case the husband has the superficial reputation of being a most generous provider and a good husband. In almost every case the man is proud of having his wife and daughters dress well and entertain lavishly.

Quite frequently this generous provider is extravagant in the matter of expensive foods, wines, garments, and jewels; but while he pays his bills without comment and asks no retrenchment, he becomes a miser and a slaveholder the moment his wife asks for a purse of her own or a regular allowance for her personal needs.

It seems almost incredible that such a condition can exist to-day in our land of opulence, and among people who are supposed to be cultured and progressive, and where woman is considered to be queen in her own realm.

Yet this condition *does exist* to an amazing extent. It is one cause of the growth of the Equal

Franchise party, and invariably where it exists the men who are the home misers are violently opposed to allowing woman the vote.

These men are relics of an old-fashioned system which must give way before the march of progress —an old system where woman was regarded as a cross between a child and a grown person of arrested mentality, and where, instead of being man's helpmate and comrade, she was merely his legal chattel and upper servant of his household.

With the increase of wealth and the changed conditions of living he has ceased to think of her in this light; but, while he regards her with sufficient pride to wish her to be well cared for, well appareled, and well waited on, he has not been able to understand her nature sufficiently to trust her with money or to realize the indelicacy of his treatment of her in this respect. The daily humiliation which many refined wives endure in the matter of money makes the position of their servants seem enviable to them.

There can be no romance, no sentiment, no happy love life, and no mutual respect between man and wife without financial independence and complete trust in money matters. If a woman shows a tendency to use money unwisely it should be the duty of the husband to train her in business methods.

There is no better training for a woman in this matter than having an allowance and understanding that all her personal needs must be provided for on a stated sum. Once supplied with this allowance, she should ask no favors beyond, and should be asked no questions regarding her use of it.

The man who compels his wife to ask for every penny she uses is not a credit to any country, and is undeserving the name of a good American.

XXIV

SEX

Over and over we came this way,
  For just one purpose; oh, stubborn Soul,
Turn with a will to your work to-day
  And learn the lesson of Self-Control.

PERSONS of large intellect, who have given years of their lives to profound study of life and all its mysteries, make bold to assert that long and long ago, in a prehistoric period, there was but one sex. Yet that one sex was bi-sexual, both man and woman; and when that race occupied the plane of manifestation beings were created by other laws than those which now govern nature.

Gradually the masculine element in some of these beings began to be accented, the feminine element in others; and so, after many eons of time, the two separate sexes were established.

At first the all-male creature or the all-female was regarded as some strange specimen, a distortion, an abnormal creation. But gradually they increased in numbers until they became universal.

And then followed all the evils of sex excesses

and abuses which have made so much trouble in the world ever since and have about culminated in the present Iron Age of the earth.

And now, it is said, the pendulum is beginning to swing back toward the bi-sexual standard again as the growing tendency of masculinity of the female and the growing femininity of the male indicate.

And all this is watched over by the Great Lords of Karma, who have given souls this experience in order that they may learn by pain and suffering the folly of seeking for happiness in any paths which lead away from the spiritual.

One of the first evils of the sex separation showed itself in the two distinct codes of morals established for men and women who broke the laws of the world in sexual matters.

Through some strange course of reasoning it was supposed that the feminine being must be all chastity, all virtue, all spirituality, and wholly beyond and above temptation of any kind, and that she must be kept in ignorance of sex matters until she was a wife and mother. Yet she must prove perfect in both relations and fill those positions with unerring skill and wisdom.

Meantime the man was expected to be sensual and polygamous, to make and break his own laws, to follow his impulses and use no self-control, because he was a man, and to be forgiven and accepted by society at large, no matter what his record.

Then the race began to study into laws of heredity, and it was observed that daughters more frequently resembled the father than the mother and that they quite as frequently inherited the father's nature as his features, and some inquiring minds asked why the daughter of the sensual, pleasure-loving father, who was the living image of her sire, should be expected to grow into a miracle of modesty and virtue without any guide from her parents or society or any special effort made in her behalf, but merely on the supposition that she was protected by her sex, or why she should be punished more severely than man if she failed.

Some wise minds of an inquiring tendency are asking that question every year, and more minds of a conventional mold are finding it a difficult question to answer. Gradually it is being borne in upon the public consciousness that men and women are created by the same powers and with the same tendencies and emotions and passions and temptations, and that they should be protected and judged by the same laws. Gradually, but very, very slowly, the trend of public opinion is toward a larger view in these matters of sex.

It is a curious thing that the Christian Church has been so very tardy in making the path of the repentant woman sinner easier, since of all sinners mentioned by Christ the Master, He was most lenient toward the Magdalen and the woman taken in adultery.

His most severe word toward them was, "Go, and sin no more."

It is the misfortune for the world that there is no fuller record of what He did to help them after they went forth and tried to sin no more. If the gentle Master had realized just how hard and cruel and severe His avowed disciples were to be in these later centuries toward the women who sought to reform after having fallen, He surely would have given more ample instructions for both the erring ones and the disciples.

XXV

THE POWER OF RECONSTRUCTION

Oh, great this age; its mighty work is *Man*—
Knowing himself the universal life;
And great our faith which shows itself in works
For human freedom and for racial good.

YOU can reconstruct your life, no matter what your environment, physically, mentally, and morally, as well as financially, if you will.

If you came into the world with weak lungs and anemic blood, it will require more effort for you to become robust than for some well-born, virile child who has only to breathe and frolic to keep in health. But you can do it if you will practise deep breathing and learn what not to eat and drink and insist upon your right to all the health and vigor of the universe.

I have met and talked with a hale and hearty woman of sixty whose family all passed away with consumption and who was herself expected to die in her "teens." She resolved to live, however, and began to breathe. She devoted half an hour three times a day to deep breathing in the open air. At first it caused violent coughing-spells, but they grew less frequent as she persisted. She lived outdoors as much as possible and slept in a well-ventilated room. She put compresses of cold water on her chest for an hour every night and began taking cold sponge-baths until she was strong enough to indulge in cold tub-baths.

She gave up pastry, fine bread, tea and coffee, and ate no pork. She drank nothing at her meals, but copiously of fresh spring water and good creamy milk between meals. She practised gentle calisthenics every day, increasing their force as she gained in strength; and night and day she thought health for herself and believed she was to become robust. She realized her expectation —married, and was the mother of strong children, whom she began to train in their infancy to breathe and exercise properly, to live out of doors, and to bathe in cold water.

There is no evil power, no evil inheritance, no cruel environment, which can hinder or circumvent a strong and determined soul seeking for health, usefulness, truth, and success.

Keep that fact well in mind and live to it, no matter what the whole world may say to the contrary. Fear nothing. You are a part of the splendid universe, and you are here to get the best out of this phase of life. You can do this only by developing the very finest qualities in yourself and by controlling whatever is unworthy and unwholesome and disagreeable. Be well and strong, because sickness is disagreeable for yourself and to others. I repeat, health is the simplest thing in life if you breathe, eat, exercise, and think properly. It requires no aid of any one if you will be faithful in these things.

Be industrious.

You were put on earth to do your share of work, and idleness is a sin. Do something even if you cannot at once do the work you prefer; and all the time assert that your right employment is coming to you. It will come. Look for something to be thankful and glad over each day, and you will find it. Consider each disappointment and trouble as so much experience and as a temporary lesson set for you to learn. When it seems insupportable, as these things do at first, go alone by yourself, sit down, and take a few deep inhalations, and say, "I am breathing in the benefit and strength and wisdom which this experience was meant to bestow upon me." After five minutes of this thought and practice you will go forth with calmness and new strength to face the world. Cast out every bitter and resentful thought. Nothing of worth can be achieved by you in any line while your vital forces are vitiated by anger, revenge, or hatred.

Let the Great Lawmaker of the universe adjust things. All you need to do is to make yourself a receptacle for His love and power to do good in the world and to your fellow-men. If any one does evil to you, pass on your way without fear or malice. No one can harm you if you do not harm yourself by retaliation.

Fill your soul and mind so full of love and sympathy and joy that nothing lesser can find accommodation. Once you do this you are immune from disaster. Sorrow will find you, but not misfortune. Evil cannot touch you, and blessings will follow you.

You are Master of your Destiny.

If we sit down and center our thoughts on the tip of the tongue for fifteen minutes every day we shall soon be conscious of an increased sense of taste. If we center them on hope we shall find hopefulness coming. If we compel the mind to turn away from unpleasant topics, and by assertion and reiteration of assertions teach it to think joy and health and happiness and success we are producing those conditions for ourselves.

God has filled an immense storehouse called the Universe with all good things. He wants us to possess them. He has made us His heirs. Just so surely as we will believe this and assert it and think it, no matter what darkness and poverty we are in, conditions will change, and we will come into our own little by little.

This cannot be done instantaneously by one who has to contend against a lifelong habit of despondent thought, but it can be done by persistency and practice. It is the law and "is good for one and good for all."

XXVI

THE LAW OF JUSTICE

You are your own devil, you are your own God.
You fashioned the paths that your footsteps have trod.
And no one can save you from error or sin
Until you shall hark to the spirit within.

WHATEVER you are here on earth, whatever you possess, you have in some life earned. And upon you, and you alone, depends your next situation. If you have poverty and ill health and you are determined to improve your condition by industry, economy, and sensible living, though you may die before you attain your aim, still you have laid the spiritual foundation for a better fortune and a better body in the next incarnation.

If you have longed for education and accomplishment, if you have struggled to obtain them, every effort you make will be placed to your credit when you come again.

If you have beauty, talent, wealth, and are not making good use of them—use which will benefit others and leave the race better off for your having lived—then you will be obliged to return without beauty, without talent, without wealth, and work your way back to divine favor.

This great law of cause and effect is called karma. We are all making good or bad karma every hour.

The fair working-girl who is turning away from the temptation to wear fine apparel at the cost of her self-respect, and who is seeing herself grow faded and care-worn while she toils to support an old mother or a little sister, is called good karma. She is preparing a beautiful body and fair raiment and a happy environment for herself in the next incarnation.

The companion who laughs at her while she drives by in her "protector's" motor-car is making bad karma. She is preparing an ugly or deformed body for herself when she comes again, a body which will not be attractive to vice, and she will have to do the toil she has refused to do here. There is no escaping the law of karma, which is the law of justice.

If you have been educated on traditional lines, you are thinking that the Creator of this vast universe makes each soul from new material and sends it to quicken the unborn child at a certain period.

If you think anything at all about the matter beyond that you must wonder why one of these God-made souls is sent into a palace, another into the slums.

If you decide that some are made to suffer and

be poor and unfortunate on earth in order that they shall shine above their affluent brothers after they go to heaven, then you must think the Creator a very partial and unjust being, or He would not show such favoritism. Any way you reason it out you will find the whole matter incompatible with justice unless you accept the idea of reincarnation.

Briefly told, the idea is, that the Great Power which made the universe has always existed and will always exist. And all that exists has always existed, and every soul that animates the body of any human being to-day has animated the bodies of innumerable beings over and over again.

It is, of course, a very vast thought. But the idea is not one whit more difficult to grasp than the modern one, that each soul is made out of new material and that the beginning of life was a few thousand years ago. It is easier to imagine a circle without beginning and without end than a straight line which begins nowhere.

The creative power is so vast that it is almost unthinkable. But we have to accept that as a fact. And it is so magnificent and stupendous a fact that it thrills the mind and heart and soul, unless all are atrophied or undeveloped. This earth is only one of millions of worlds more wonderful, and we are but expressions of that vast power. Everything that exists anywhere is divine. There is nothing which is not an expression of what we call God.

In the course of eons of time we have occupied many bodies and many worlds; and we are in this world what our former lives made us. We will be in our next incarnation just what we are now preparing ourselves to be.

The law governing this universe is the law of cause and effect. If in some former existence you lived a life of luxury and license, if you "trod flowery paths of dalliance" and ignored the voice of reason and wisdom, then you are back in this world for the purpose of working out your debt to the universe. You are poor, frail of body, and between you and health and success and comfort and happiness lie seemingly insurmountable obstacles. You look on other more fortunate human beings and wonder why God has been so unkind to you.

But you have made your own destiny. And now you possess the power to change that destiny. You can change it to a wonderful degree, here and now; and you can build a glorious destiny for your next coming.

It is possible that your next life will be spent on some other planet; but wherever you go, the character you are now making will shape your destiny. Besides this, there are intervening "heavens" and "hells," through which we must pass and in which we must dwell, according to our desserts, and each thought and act of your life here is determining what your experiences in those planes of existence will be. Modern creeds have taught the selfish, mercenary, and self-indulgent woman that when she dies, asking God to forgive her sins, she will immediately join the spirit of her lovely child who passed away in early youth. But such a woman has not made such a reunion possible. She will have to earn her admission before she will be admitted to the realm where her child dwells.

Those who think hate and envy and malice, those who live wholly and only for the enjoyment of the senses, must seek their own kind in the intervening realms. Spiritual birds of a feather flock together, as well as the earth birds. This consciousness should act as a mighty stimulus to persistent and patient efforts at self-conquest and self-development—conquest of the unworthy and weak and indolent impulses, development of the worthy and strong and aspiring side of our natures.

For every such effort means a step forward toward realization of our ideal and its absolute attainment, either here or elsewhere.

XXVII

THE BUSINESS OF LIFE

Forth from little motes in Chaos
  We have come to what we are;
And no evil force can stay us—
  We shall mount from star to star.

LIFE means action, from the cradle to the funeral pile.

The situation into which we are born and our mental and physical equipments at birth are the result of past actions in other lives, and all our actions while here are forming conditions for lives to come. There are limitless possibilities in this life to overcome, whatever conditions hamper or annoy us, and to bring into realization whatever hopes or aspirations lure us. We have not begun to sound the depths in our minds.

The most brilliant, the most studious, the most reverent, the most persistent have only sailed about the shores of this great ocean; they have not even imagined what deep waters lie beyond and what rare pearls lie under those deep waters. But we have shining examples of individuals who have achieved so much under such discouraging conditions that their lives become an inspiration to all who meditate upon them.

Lincoln, born in poverty, reared in the same hard school, surrounded by the commonplace and the undesirable, and deprived of all opportunities for advancement, made himself a colossal figure in the eyes of centuries to come through high thinking, clean living, and the persistent cultivation of the old immortal virtues of honesty, truth, courage, and unselfishness and devotion to those duties which stood nearest.

All his thoughts, all his ambitions, all his actions, from childhood to maturity, were directed toward the attainment of those virtues and their practical application to every issue which life presented. Unconsciously to himself, he was treading the path to immortal fame; he was building a character which would invite tremendous responsibilities and creating the strength to meet them grandly.

He knew what life meant. It meant action and achievement through growth.

There is no such thing as inaction during this life. We are continually going forward or backward.

You are either stronger or weaker this year than you were last year.

You are braver or more cowardly.

You are more hopeful or more pessimistic.

You are more capable mentally or less so.

You have better or poorer command of your forces.

You have more efficiency or not as much.

You are nearer your goal or farther from it.

You are a better human being or not as good.

Next year at this time you will be still farther onward or still farther backward.

Every thought, every word, and every act of each day is chiseling out the statue you are making of yourself.

If you desire to be an expression of the Creator's finest handiwork, you must work with care.

Delicate tools are these thoughts of ours, and they must be used with caution.

Every morning say to yourself (the Self self): "To-day I will think of whatever is beautiful, strong, noble, wholesome, and worthy. I will entertain hope, courage, reverence, gratitude, and love as the guests of my heart. I will make thoughts of health at ease in the guest-chamber of my mind, so dis-ease may not enter. I will achieve something worth while in my chosen field of endeavor. I will work faithfully, but I will find time to sit alone with thoughts of my Creator for a little while, and no worldly ambition or anxiety shall intrude upon that time."

Just as surely as you carry out your days along these lines, just as surely shall the true meaning of life come to you, and you shall know God, and you shall know that the meaning of life *is* God and that in Him are all the things for which you long: Health, Happiness, Prosperity, Usefulness, Beauty, and Joy.

And you shall know that the earth is not a vale of tears, but a great and beautiful preparatory school where the soul of man is sent to study and learn its divinity and to develop its wonderful powers.

XXVIII

THE WASTE OF THOUGHT-FORCE

Life is too short for aught but high endeavor—
Too short for hate, but long enough for love.

WHILE anger, if frequently indulged, is a destructive use of mental force and a waste of energy, it has been claimed that an occasional burst of anger is better for the system than a state of dull lethargy. We are assured that emotion and enthusiasm are necessary aids to a good circulation, and to the ensuing perfect action of the human mechanism, physical and mental; and that it is better to be roused into anger than never to be roused at all.

But anger is a tonic which must be sparingly employed, or the result will prove disastrous. The individual who is easily and perpetually roused to a display of anger is wasting the precious substance of his mind and receiving nothing in return. It is as if he flung money to the four winds of the compass, in a mood of lawless defiance. Yet the most hopeless and exasperating type of mental spendthrift on earth is the whiner.

The man or woman who is for ever complaining

of the hard lot which has been dealt out by Destiny, and who has developed a mania for sympathy, is hour by hour, and day by day, and year by year wasting the most precious inheritance a human being possesses and inviting spiritual poverty. Two women in one town were brought face to face with the consciousness that upon them depended the maintenance of their homes and the future of their children. Both women had been unfortunate in the marriage lottery, and both had drawn blanks—men without moral sense or any realization of their responsibilities to keep their marriage vows and to support their families.

Both women turned from the shelter of the home they had enjoyed for a period of years and entered the arena of the world's workers. One turned with a smiling face and the poise of a philosopher; the other entered the new field with a whining voice and ever-teary eyes. The one began to relate her first steps toward upward success and to talk of the hopeful future; the other wept over the dark present and recounted the useless tale of the better days she had previously enjoyed. The first woman made friends and continually enlarged her sphere of action; the other drove people from her with her whining voice and melancholy face and went from failure to failure; and each failure gave her new themes of melancholy conversation. Always she wondered why the other woman was so lucky and she so unlucky. Little by little her mental energies and creative forces were dissipated in the most useless manner.

The first woman kept the weak husband from going utterly to ruin and awoke in him a sense of his own unworthiness; the other woman widened the breach hopelessly and gave the outside world an opportunity to say, "It is no wonder the man went wrong; such a woman would drive any man away."

It was a whining woman who inspired a young genius, Thomas Dreler, to formulate a wonderful prayer. He had been in close association with the wife of an acquaintance, a woman who was always complaining that she did not "feel well" and that life did not move to her liking; from week-end to week-end she was seeking for sympathy. When this woman had gone, Mr. Dreler, who is a bachelor of twenty-five, made this prayer:

A MAN'S PRAYER

Give me, God, a vibrant flame of a woman for a mate. Make her, I pray Thee, a woman of merriment. Fill her with a master love for the strenuous. Enlarge her vision so that it will see all things, and make her wise with that wisdom which shall see naught that demands her forgiveness. Give her a body compounded with strength and symmetry. Send surging through her a spirit elemental. Fill her with a love for the open air, the high hills, the winding streams, the storms that send snow and sleet across the wastes. Make her vibrate with the joy of the lightning-flash and the crash of the thunder. Let her ever be a silent worshiper of the stars. I would have her frank and fearless and gentle—fit to play her hand in the Game of Life in the manner of a master. And when in Thy goodness Thou hast given this woman unto me, let me ever find in her something elusive—something that shall ever keep me searching joyously with wonder. Give me, God, a woman who will demand more of me than I have ever dared to demand of myself, who will help me liberate that creative energy necessary for the realization of my dreams. If it be Thy will that this woman be not given to me in the flesh, give her to me as an ideal woman who will lead me daily to render to my neighbors the service most expressive of my great love for her, and may she never permit me to find the final goal.

Waste of thought is the most common waste which exists, and there is no other extravagance so devastating in its results.

For thought is the God-given power which was meant for man to use constructively, and to have, and be, and do whatever he wished.

If you are a merchant, waste no time or breath in talking about the dishonesty and unworthiness of your rivals in business.

If you are a physician, or a beauty specialist, or a dressmaker, or teacher of wisdom, the same advice applies to you. All the vitality you can draw from space keep to make your own methods successful.

Each time you indulge in criticism and backbiting or in open denunciation of the methods of some competitor you are losing ground yourself.

Let other artists paint, let other authors write,

other merchants sell, other actors act, and other singers sing. Wish them all glory, success, happiness. Lift your soul to the vastness of space and refuse to be petty and small and jealous and critical. Ask for all the force, all the light, all the wisdom that is being stored up for your use. Receive it, and go your way.

I have known a physician to devote the greater part of his time while calling on patients, or while they were in his institution, to the disparagement of brother doctors whose ideas did not coincide with his own.

There are metaphysicians who are similarly inclined, even though such a procedure is in contradiction of the laws they teach. But, while it is a simple matter to teach philosophy, it is very difficult to make it a part of our daily working habits.

Every time we stop in our appeal to the forces within or without for strength and aid, to criticize a fellow-man who follows some other line of procedure, we turn off the current the Divine Electrician has always in working order for our use.

There is room for every sincere soul on God's earth. No one can crowd another. No one can injure another's business. You alone can injure or interfere with your own affairs, and the surest way to do it is to interfere with the affairs of another.

Wish every man godspeed. No matter if he opens a place of business next door to you in direct competition with you, wish him godspeed. Say to him and say to yourself, "There is room for good workers everywhere. We are like two stars in space, and one does not interfere with the other's light. We only give the world more light."

It may be hard work to bring yourself into this state of mind, but once you arrive there you will be conscious of new power, new force.

If your competitor is on a lower plane and opened his business merely to injure you, rest assured this attitude of your mind will have tenfold the power to overcome his efforts that a resentful and defiant one would have.

Conserve your forces. Nothing dissipates them like flaw-picking. Think about your own splendid possibilities and let your mind reach out for new ideas and new developments in what you are doing, not back and down, seeking flaws in what your competitors are doing.

XXIX

HEALTH AND BEAUTY

Affirm the body, beautiful and whole,
The earth-expression of immortal soul.

WE must submit with such good grace as we can to the eternal story of human ills.

The tale of "hard colds" and "threatened with pneumonia" and "almost bronchitis" and all the miserable train of attendant maladies is constantly rehearsed by friends, strangers, and casual acquaintances, and we must listen and show a certain amount of sympathy or be deemed brutal. But we can at least resolve to return good for evil, and not relate your own ailments to every passer-by.

If we keep our minds filled with the thought of *perfect radiant health* it will do much toward helping us realize that blessing.

To fill our lungs full, *full* of fresh air slowly, many times each day, and to say, "I am health absolute," and to picture ourselves as vigorous and full of vitality, is a long step toward resistance of disease.

"As a man thinketh, so is he," and if we refuse to entertain the fear of disease and persist in drawing mind pictures of health we are well equipped to meet most weather emergencies.

But if we do not possess the mental poise at all times to ward off sickness, at least let us refuse to spread thought germs of disease by continually talking sickness. We can stay at home and send for a doctor if we do not know how to get well without him, and we can, if we will, keep still about our experience afterward. Life is too short to waste it talking disease.

Your life depends on your breathing, and therefore it is first necessary to learn to take deep, full breaths instead of half filling the lungs, and therefore not infusing sufficient oxygen into the blood to keep it in good, healthy condition. Correct breathing is absolutely necessary. The man who thinks rightly, who breathes thoroughly, and who does not eat too much has the secret of health pretty well in his possession.

If he falls ill, it will be but a temporary illness. Many people imagine a hearty appetite a road to health. It is far more frequently a short cut to the grave. Few human beings die of starvation, many of gluttony, still more of indigestible food.

There is a young woman who is taking most scientific care of her person in order to preserve her beauty. She is young, in the very morning of life, and nature gave her beautiful features and complexion and form.

She studies the fashions and plans becoming

costumes, and she patronizes the "specialists" who know how to beautify and preserve the skin and hair and nails and figure.

She takes physical exercises to keep her body supple, and all this is sensible and wise. The body is the soul's temple and should be cared for.

But the most important factor in feminine beauty this young woman has utterly neglected—the mind. She neither reads nor studies.

Worse still, she harbors resentful thoughts toward her friends and acquaintances for the least offense, or what she imagines an offense. Unless her associates agree with her on all matters she assumes a haughty and cold air and sets her face in a frozen mold that, unconsciously to herself, is day by day ruining her beauty. All her friends see and realize the fact. The eyes are becoming hard, the mouth petulant, the whole expression disagreeable, the whole woman unbearable. Added to this, she is self-indulgent and uses no control in the matter of appetite, and that fault is making more ravage upon her beauty than all the specialists can remedy.

Even a plain woman who begins at eighteen to cultivate the mind and heart and soul can be beautiful at thirty.

And at forty she will be still more beautiful, and will attract the admiration of all eyes, where the sculptured face, with cruel or cold heart and uncultivated mind, will pass unnoticed.

I saw an old lady close to her seventies once

with the most exquisite mouth—it was as soft as a child's, with sweetly molded corners and sympathetic curves to the lips, and the whole expression was suggestive of the magical word—Love.

A dozen young women in the room would pass without attracting the attention this charming old lady won.

Angels of goodness and amiability in the way of sweet thoughts and worthy habits had chiseled that mouth. Every thought, every emotion, every impulse, leaves its mark upon the face, and the most beautiful features cannot make a beautiful woman at twenty-five or thirty if the mind previous to that time has been ruled by anger, revenge, petulance, selfishness, and indolence.

The woman who is for ever trying to convince the public how young she is expresses one extreme of folly, and the woman who is constantly telling how old she is illustrates another.

There are women who are so extremely sensitive upon the subject of advancing years that they hasten to announce each birthday from the housetop, lest some one should attempt to remind them of it.

"I am no longer young," "I am quite an old woman," are phrases one hears now and then from the women whose faces belie their words; but, fortunately, this type of woman is becoming rarer, for the new philosophy is teaching the world that the mind, rather than the years, create age and its appearance. In this day, too, we but rarely see the wife who looks old enough to be her husband's mother while yet his junior; at least, we do not encounter her in the large centers, where life is full of variety and action. In the country places she is still to be found—the faded, care-worn woman of forty, whose spruce, up-to-date husband a few years older might well pass for her son.

She knows how old she looks, and the knowledge frets and worries her and adds new lines to her face.

She does not know that she is herself in fault for letting her mind run on thoughts of the passing years, and in a belief that her youth and her charms are vanished.

Time was when a married woman donned a cap and a sober air and "settled down," even though she were in her "teens."

In those days husbands delighted in calling their wives "mother" or "the old lady," according to their mood, and society allowed no margin for youthful spirits after the wedding vows were taken. Yet it found excuses for the gallant husband who remained young while his wife advanced into premature age and unloveliness.

The married woman to-day has every legitimate avenue for pleasure and distraction which is open to the débutante; and she is expected to adorn herself as becomingly as does her single sister, while as a rule she has a much better furnished mind and is more entertaining to both men and women than the average young girl.

In this age nothing is more absurd than for a woman to imagine her power to please and attract her husband and hold her own socially has ceased because she has attained middle life.

The woman of brain and culture who has the self-control and the perseverance to combat obesity, and the mental and scientific equipment to defy wrinkles, should feel no fear of advancing time—should, indeed, regard it as a generous friend, with added gifts to bestow.

In every age there have been examples of mature women who have held their sway socially and sentimentally. Cleopatra, Helen of Troy, Aspasia were all women who had seen twoscore years when their greatest prowess was felt. Josephine was forty years old before she became empress, and her sway was supreme and her beauty pre-eminent at that age.

Madame de Maintenon was advanced in years and not at all beautiful when she captured a king for a husband, and held him captive till he died.

At an American army post one season a new belle appeared, so full of wit and so sympathetic and so entertaining, as well as so lovely in person, that from staid generals down to boyish recruits all hearts were laid at her feet.

She charmed her own sex as readily as she did men, as do all really fascinating women; yet it was a woman, I believe, who discovered through some chance mutual acquaintance, and who did not delay in reporting the surprising fact, that the charmer was past fifty years of age.

It is not the mere preservation of beauty which gives such women their power; it is sympathy, tact, adaptability, and a knowledge of human nature, and a desire to please.

All are qualities worth cultivating.

XXX

SELF-CONTROL

For this alone the Universe exists—
That man may find himself is Destiny.

It is not so important that things go as I think they should as it is that I should be master of them through self-control.—*Unity.*

YOU can apply this in any kind of experience you may have. If you are working among people whose manners and habits jar upon you, apply this rule and watch developments.

Once you *control yourself* you will be surprised to find how many things which annoy you will change or disappear.

Just so long as you are a servant to your own irritable nerves and whims you will find the world is one succession of sharp corners against which you bruise yourself at every move. When you become master of yourself the corners will round into curves imperceptibly but surely.

The same rule applies in your home.

What attitude are you taking toward your own family and relatives and friends and toward humanity?

Are you posing as a martyr? Do you wear the resigned expression of a wronged creature who must submit to persecution, or a sullen, resentful one, or a belligerent one?

Are you thinking and brooding over your wrongs and making yourself and others miserable in consequence?

If you are doing any one of these things you are a criminal—far worse than many a convict behind prison bars. If you are disturbing the peace of your household, the comfort of husband or children or relatives or friends by your temper, your complaints, or your sarcasm, then you are a murderess. It is a more unpardonable crime than many committed by people who are condemned by judge and jury, no matter how high your standing in church or community. No woman is a really good woman unless she is an agreeable woman to her daily associates.

Perhaps you are a wronged, misused wife, and tell me your troubles have destroyed your nervous system and that you cannot help being irritable and cross and saying unpleasant things at times.

I tell you in reply that the most adorable, agreeable, and angelic woman I ever knew was a wronged wife, a woman who had suffered every indignity and humiliation and neglect possible from a mean, brutal-natured man. Yet she made a heaven for her children and friends in her home.

She had learned this great law of becoming Master of Circumstances through self-control.

Although things about her were not to her liking, she made all these things seem as trifles before her calm self-conquest. She said to herself, "Though my best love and my best faith and my sweetest hopes have been thrown into the dust, I will not let myself go down.

"I have lost respect for the man to whom I gave my life's happiness, but I will not lose respect for myself; and I will show the world I can create happiness, even if I cannot find it where I hoped it would be, in my marital life."

Surely this was better than becoming soured, aggressive, complaining, and pessimistic, and making her presence dreaded by all her associates.

There was a great French writer who said, "If you have not what you like, like what you have."

But even if you cannot like your environment, you can make yourself a *master* of it, and refuse absolutely to be dominated by it. You can grow and rise above it; and after a time, if you do this, the environment will change and circumstances will alter to your will.

The whole philosophy of life is contained in that little sentence from *Unity*.

"*It is not so important that things go as I think they should as it is that I should be master of them by self-control.*"

XXXI

THE SPRINGS OF HAPPINESS

What sunny roads of happiness lead out
Beyond the realms of indolence and doubt!

WHAT is happiness?

Is happiness within the reach of the average person?

Is happiness desirable?

If happiness were possible, would not a great incentive to human endeavor be removed?

What is the chief aim of life?

Happiness is the state of mind which enables us to be grateful for the boon of life and to rejoice with the rising of each sun that another day has dawned for our use.

Happiness is within the reach of every individual who is willing to develop his higher qualities and to control his lower and more selfish nature. Not until he realizes that this is the foundation of happiness, however, can we hope for this effort on the part of the average human being.

The great majority of people imagine happiness means possession of whatever the human heart craves or the human mind desires. A very little observation will prove to the most casual thinker how erroneous is that conception of the word. Some of our multimillionaires are in possession of whatever they desire, but it would be unwise to point to any one as a happy man.

The child with its toys on Christmas morning, the lover and maid in their first bliss, the young bride and groom, the mother with her first-born, the girl at her first ball, all are happy in one sense of the word. But it is an ephemeral and feverish happiness oftentimes, and, besides, it walks the specter of fear and the ogre of change.

The toys are broken; the lovers are tormented with jealousy; the bride and groom and the young mother fear death or disaster; and the young girl is succeeded by a rival belle at her second ball, and happiness dwells no longer beside any of these. The man who makes a fortune by the rise of stocks is happy for a day; the warrior who receives a decoration for bravery and the scholar who carries away the honors of his class are happy.

But these are all passing conditions, not settled states of mind, and they cannot be called happiness absolute.

Real happiness must rest on the foundation of unselfishness. It must spring from the consciousness of usefulness, and it must be one with Faith. It must forget its own goal in helping others to find theirs. Only this kind of happiness is desirable.

The happiness which means gratified ambition

and appetites is not a high and noble aim for any soul to seek. And gratified ambitions and satisfied appetites do not result in happiness, but in satiety and discontent. If such happiness were possible, then, indeed, a great incentive to human endeavor would be removed; for it is the ceaseless striving toward other goals than the one achieved which spurs men on to new effort.

The chief aim of life is regarded by thousands of people as the attainment of happiness—personal gratifications.

The chief and only aim of life intended by the great Creator is the perfecting of character, the bringing out of the God within. The moment a human being grasps this fact he is on the road to happiness. For whatever sorrowful experience comes to him he will turn it toward self-development and find his happiness in the knowledge that he is working toward self-completion.

Only when a man knows that he can never be happy in doing one act or harboring one thought which can lower him mentally or morally, or can mar the life of another, is he on the right road to real happiness. Wealth, so eagerly and madly pursued by the majority of men, has little to do with happiness.

Idleness is an absolute foe to happiness.

No idle man or woman has any comprehension of the word. Work, regarded by many as the *curse* sent upon man for sin, is instead God's highway to the hills of *happiness*.

Not drudgery, but blessed employment, which brings all the activities into play and gives a zest to recreation.

Wealth, fame, power, success, position, beauty —all of these are incapable of producing happiness unless the soul is set toward the heights of God and the heart filled with the attributes of the *Christ*—love and sympathy.

Happiness would be impossible were any one being left alone on earth; and just to the degree that a soul is separated from the rest of humanity by selfishness and lack of universal sympathy, so is that soul incapable of enjoying happiness while still pursuing it. Just in the measure we feel near to our kind and eager to be of use are we augmenting our chances for happiness on earth.

Only he who finds such happiness on earth can expect to find it in heaven. For happiness is a mental state and can be fashioned by our thoughts. The approach to heaven is through the pathway of happiness. The approach to happiness lies in love, trust, and service.

Love for the universe, trust in God, and service to humanity.

And this leads to the happiness which is immortal. The happiness "within the reach of all"— the happiness which is "desirable," and the happiness which is "the chief aim of life."

XXXII

THE ART OF BECOMING POPULAR

Over and over and over,
These truths I will say and sing,
  That love is mightier far than hate,
  That a man's own thought is a man's own fate,
And that life is a goodly thing.

TO be popular in the world of art is, according to the canons of the "high-brow critic," to be a dweller outside of the inner sanctuary.

Yet the Sermon on the Mount is popular.

Whatever possesses all the qualities of real greatness must be popular, even though things which possess no qualities of greatness may be widely popular also.

The large majority of people may like something mediocre, and only few may like something which contains many of the elements of greatness—something too fine for the masses to comprehend—but that which possesses *all* the elements of greatness must reach and grip the whole race. For among those elements simplicity and sympathy must be counted, those opening wedges to all minds.

The human being who is popular is sometimes accused of being all things to all men, and there is a cant phrase much in vogue among the unpopular about "caring only for a few people and being cared for by only a few." And this serves frequently as an easy excuse for the unpopularity of the dull or the disagreeable.

To be a popular individual in any community of self-respecting and morally disposed citizens, and to grow in popularity with acquaintance and time, calls for nobility of character, purity of purpose, and kindness of heart.

It calls also for tact, for discretion, for good judgment, for unselfishness, for generosity, for amiability, and the power to bring out the best in others. It calls for a heart big enough to rejoice in the achievements of others. It calls for the elimination of all jealousy, all tendencies to gossip, all impulses to be indolent or indifferent or self-centered.

Therefore it would seem that an ambition to be popular is at the same time an ambition to become a worth-while individual and a practical Christian.

The man who sets out to be a great discoverer in science or a great creator in the world of art may not have the time to become a popular man in his own social circle. But if he is decidedly unpopular he is sure to lack some of the large elements of character which are necessary to bring him to the summit of the heights he seeks.

Unless he is liked and respected by those who know him best something is amiss with the man.

There is a cheap and temporary popularity which comes from the ability to amuse others, from the propensity to be generous to the limit of extravagance, and to be ever ready with unmeaning flattery, but the reign of these social leaders and lions is always brief.

Sincerity and tact are two qualities which make for lasting popularity—sincerity in thought and purpose, tact in the application of that virtue.

The tactful person knows when and how to be silent.

Many sincere individuals think a brutal expression of the most unpleasant and disagreeable opinions is an evidence of their sincerity. But the tactful man or woman knows when to speak and when to be still and how to change a topic of conversation when some one has trodden on delicate ground.

The woman who desires to be popular should first of all learn the charm which lies in listening well; and she should cultivate the art of drawing others out, of making those with whom she is thrown shine to their best advantage.

If a man talks well, lead him to converse; if he sings well, induce him to sing; and to bring forth the most attractive qualities and accomplishments of her women friends is a sure way for any woman to take a long step forward on the road to popularity.

Such a woman, possessing no marked accomplishments herself, and without beauty or great mental gifts, stands a far better chance of becoming popular than the self-conscious Venus or the prodigy of brilliant attainments who only enjoys herself when occupying the center of the social stage and basking in the glare of the spot-light.

Unselfishness, then, is the keynote to popularity, as it is the key to the highest moral worth. But this unselfishness must be mingled with good sense, with tact, with delicacy and refinement, in order to serve as an aid to popularity.

Without these ingredients unselfishness and generosity sometimes become obtrusive, officious, and offensive.

The most perfect type of popular woman is she who can shine like the sun when sunshine is needed, yet who, like that orb, does not always shine, but retires behind the clouds and calls attention to the brilliancy of the stars and the moon; one who can be entertaining or amusing or instructive, as occasion demands, but who can always put herself in the background in order to exhibit the graces and charms of others, and who is ever ready to rejoice in another's success without any belittling clause affixed to praise; one who can be tolerant of the ideas and opinions of others while holding entirely opposite ones, and who knows how to hold fast to her own ideals while understanding how others may fail to do so.

The popular woman has quick perceptions, and, however great her vogue, she is never blinded by conceit to such an extent that she fails to perceive her own faults or neglects correcting them once she sees them.

That which she finds disagreeable in others she decides to avoid doing herself.

And those graces and qualities which appeal to her in others she cultivates.

To seek popularity for the sake of being popular means the undermining of character.

To seek it through a desire to be a benefit, a pleasure, and a comfort to humanity means the building of character.

XXXIII

LIFE'S GRAY DAYS

And only the eye that has looked on snows
Can see all the beauty that lies in a rose.

AN occasional gray mood comes to the sunniest of natures, just as a gray day comes, even in the tropics; and if we use this gray day wisely we will be all the better for it.

When the bright sun of tropic lands is veiled by clouds one can see farther; and the landscape is more clearly discerned, because there is not the blinding dazzle of the sunlight.

So when our hearts are clouded with a passing mist of trouble or worry we sometimes see life more clearly, and look forward and about and beyond with a larger vision. I think it is a good thing now and then to grow utterly sick of ourselves, and to sit down and pull our minds and hearts and motives and actions and ambitions to pieces and dust them out as a watch-maker cleans a watch: to put them together again with care and resolve to begin all over and do better—*and then to do it.*

It is never well to rest too long in regrets of the

past, for that is over and gone and cannot be remedied. But it is well to remember the past enough to make it act as a guide and warning for the future. But moods of retrospection and regret and melancholy should be kept as luxuries, and must never become a habit. Indulged in rarely, they may serve as a tonic; but regularly followed, they become a poison.

When you are walking and carrying heavy burdens, and you grow utterly weary and fatigued, it is not well to keep staggering on. It is better to sit down and rest a bit, even if you feel as you pause that you can never go on again. After a little while you will feel more courage and you will go on. But do not sit too long.

Are you weary with trying to do your best, and have you about decided that you will give up the battle? Do you feel that nothing matters very much—that whether you succeed or fail is of small account to the world? Do you begin to think you are a very small unit in the universe, and that the best thing for you to do is just to take life as it comes and to make no effort to attain any special goal, either intellectually, morally, or financially? Are you sick of the eternal effort to be and do, and are you contemplating a renunciation of all ambition?

Well, stop and think a bit. Suppose Columbus had yielded to such a mood before he discovered America?

What if George Washington had made such a

decision in his early youth, or Benjamin Franklin, or Shakespeare, or Milton? What if Morse or Edison had given up the struggle to accomplish anything? And had Cyrus Field said he was weary of trying to gain his goal and so had let the ocean cable die a dream of imagination? What losers we would all be by it!

It is not merely you, yourself, who is to be benefited or harmed by your success or failure in life. You are to leave an influence on all who know you, no matter how humble your position may be.

Throw a pebble into the sea, and watch the disturbance of the waters; larger and larger grow the circles, and as they fade away invisible to the eye they are felt by the waves beyond our sight.

It is so with each one of us. You are affecting every life you encounter on life's journey to some degree. You will affect lives of beings yet unborn —in what way and through what sources it is impossible to tell; but, nevertheless, an invisible influence is at work connecting you with other destinies as by an unseen cord. Think of this when you are discouraged and disheartened and push ahead.

The fountain of happiness lies in the spirit of man: its flowing out through his being depends upon the condition of the heart and mind aqueducts.

If they are clogged with the mud of gloomy thoughts or the debris of petty aims or selfish desires, the divine fountain cannot flow and happiness cannot be experienced. Pleasurable emotions of a temporary nature can reach the mind from the outside, but this is not happiness.

A new costume, a new house, new equipage, or a journey will produce a passing delight and gladness, but these feelings subside when the costume loses its freshness, when the house and the equipage become old stories, and when the journey is over. Indeed, with the average mind, which depends upon "things happening" for its enjoyment, the pleasure lies almost wholly in the anticipation. The moment the longed-for event arrives disappointment arrives also.

Men toil and hoard their earnings, living in impatience until the day they have accumulated enough to go forth and purchase what they believe will be happiness. After it is purchased they sigh and say there is no such thing as happiness. But they are mistaken.

A woman longs for a fine house, and tires of it; then she longs for hotel life, and tires of it; and again she seeks happiness in travel, and does not find it, and says there is no such thing. But there is.

To obtain it we must clear the mind and heart of all obstructions and look into the clear Fountain of the Spirit. It does not matter what your religion or your belief may be—Jew, Christian, Pagan, Catholic, Protestant, Buddhist—so you realize your Oneness with the Great Cause and know that Cause is Love; and that from Love you came, and in Love you live, and to Love you must return.

Once this consciousness takes possession of you the fountain of happiness is set in action and will flood your being, even in times of sorrow and in hours of pain.

Pleasurable events, success, material gains, or gratified desires will add to your means of enjoyment; but if you are deprived of all these things, you will feel only passing disappointment; the waters of the fountain within will flow on and lave you with their gladness.

Though you fall asleep in tears, you will waken in joy. Though you meet with a thousand disappointments and are encompassed with cares, yet will you feel hope rising in your heart and the rapture of life tingling in your veins. Solitude will be a delight to you, yet will you love to mingle with your kind, knowing all are one kin.

"Great love casteth out fear." Get your heart, mind, and soul full of *love of the Creator*, and bathe your whole being in that essence, and you will discover you have found the Kingdom of Heaven. In some souls (rightly generated) this love is born. Where a man and a woman deeply, absolutely, and absorbingly love each other, and a child is the result of this love, it is usually born with a religious nature, which instinctively turns in reverence and worship toward the Creator of Universal Life.

Not all people are so born, unfortunately, and for those who are not, doubt, questioning, and despair often take the place of faith, reverence, and love. But to all such I would say, Go out and look up at the stars some clear night. Realize how many millions and billions of worlds move back beyond those which are visible to you. Think of the wonderful precision and perfection in the arrangement of the solar system, and then consider how impossible it would all be unless some stupendous intelligence conceived and planned and executed it.

Then sit down alone in your room quietly for a few moments, close your eyes, and breathe a few deep inhalations and ask the Spirit of Love and Reverence to come into your being. Be silent—breathe and wait. Free your mind of all other thoughts, just as you would empty a vessel into which one was asked to pour clear water. Think of nothing but your desire for Love and Reverence.

It will not come at one bidding if you have accustomed yourself to doubt and despondency.

But if you take a little time each day and make your mind passive, only asking for what you desire, Love and Reverence, *they will be given.* Once your mind is filled with these sentiments, *all other things shall be added.* But the strange part of it will be that you cease to care greatly for "all other things" after you find the "Kingdom of Heaven" which is in your own mind and heart.

You will be happy anywhere and under all conditions. Yet whatever is added to your life you will enjoy with a new kind of enjoyment. "Luck" will seem to come to you in many ways. You will cease to worry and fret over trivial or material matters.

You will grow strong and vital, and your tastes will be simple. You will not know what loneliness is, and your ambition will be to make the most of your own qualities rather than to win the world's acclaim. Yet, should that come to you, you will use it to the world's advantage.

Your only "fear" will be the fear of not living utterly true to the light within you—which is the light from the Source.

XXXIV

THE REVIVAL OF DANCING

When love for his Maker awoke in man
The dance began.

DANCING is an expression of joy in life. As far back as history reaches we find dancing associated with religious rites. Dancing comprises all the other arts. A beautiful dancer expresses poetry, music, sculpture, painting, all in the dance.

Besides being the most beautiful of all arts, it is the most healthful of all exercises when enjoyed under right conditions. Besides being the most healthful, it is the most moral of exercises.

Young people who are given training in dancing and allowed to dance frequently in clean, wholesome environments and under wise chaperons utilize surplus vitality, which, when suppressed by rigid rules or bigoted ideas, ofttimes results in mischief and disaster.

Take the old-fashioned religious communities where dancing is regarded as a sin, and there are always to be found numerous cases of hysteria among the young girls and various nervous maladies among the youths. No proper outlet for their superabundant young vital forces has been provided, no escape-valve.

Little children dance before they have ever seen dancing; little kittens and little puppies and all small animals dance with the joy of existence.

The waves of the sea, the leaves of the trees, the grasses of the meadow—all dance. The sunbeams dance; and light itself is ever in motion.

The man and woman who have never learned the joy to be experienced in dancing have missed a great happiness. And they have missed a means of physical grace.

The present renaissance of the art of dancing is remarkable. For a decade, at least, before the tidal wave rose, young men fled from ballrooms and left girls to find partners among themselves. The woman who had passed thirty apologized if she was seen dancing; and married people were afraid to express a love for the diversion lest they be ridiculed. A beautiful and healthful and enjoyable art seemed on the decline.

Then suddenly a change, an awakening of dull minds, a limbering of stiff joints, new life in bored faces, new interest in the oldest of all arts. The dance was reborn. And youth was reborn in the hearts and bodies and minds of men and women of all ages.

Grotesque, abnormal, unbeautiful, and even vicious were the early contortions of this reborn art. It seemed like some strange creature which had been shut in the dark so long that it became half insane when let forth once more into the full light of day. So cramped had it been with its incarceration that it flung itself about in curious contortions to make certain of its freedom.

But those contortions are now becoming graceful movements; and the insane expressions of liberty are resolving themselves once more into the primal meaning of the dance—the joy of life. Nothing more absurd, nothing more unreasonable, could be than the ban placed by various individuals on dances bearing certain names. One sees flaming head-lines announcing that somebody in power, socially or otherwise, has sent forth an edict against the tango or some other new dance.

As reasonable would it be to decry walking because it is possible to walk indecently. As reasonable would it be to brand music as an agent of the devil because music has been put to evil purposes by the vicious minded. There were certain curious dances which sprang forth like fungus growths and lasted for a night and a day, bearing unwholesome names.

The "turkey-trots" deserved to be tabooed; more particularly because of the suggestion of the barnyard and the most ungraceful of fowls, than for its own inherent wickedness. It was vulgar rather than wicked. Dancing is an art, and should suggest only the artistic and the beautiful. It belongs with perfumes, with flowers, with statuary and music, with gladness and rejoicing.

Long ago, in Eastern lands, devout and reverent souls danced songs to the rising sun; and to-day in those lands there are dancers in the temples who devote their lives to sacred rites and who live purely and sweetly that they may be worthy in the eyes of their Creator to perform the religious dances. There are moral-minded men and women who have associated every evil meaning with the word "tango." Yet the tango is graceful, artistic, and beautiful as the minuet when properly danced.

It is as innocent of anything injurious to the morals of the young as skipping the rope.

Instead of selecting some one or two new dances to decry, our well-meaning moralists should decry indecent attitudes or suggestive movements in all dancing. The same moralists make no protests against the waltz and two-step. Yet both of those dances can be made quite as objectionable as any of the most modern inventions if the participants so wish.

When the waltz was first introduced in the ballroom it created as great excitement and as violent protests as the modern dances are creating. Lord Byron, who was debarred from the pleasure by lameness, exhausted his vocabulary of invective against the immoral waltz.

Let us be sensible and reasonable. The dance is reborn, and it must live its life. It must do its work. It must be met as a factor in social life. Instead of attempting to crush it or abolish it, instead of saying to our young people, "You can dance and two-step, but you must not learn any of the new dances; they are indecent," let us say: "Learn all the new dances, but be modest, decent, graceful, and well-behaved on the dancing-floor.

"Dance only with your friends and in the environment which is respectable and safe from intrusion of the undesirable. Show all observers how beautiful a thing dancing may be."

And to our older people let us offer hearty congratulations that they no longer need apologize or explain when owning to a love of the art of all arts. For to-day the man or woman who does not dance is the exception. He or she needs to explain why. Not the dancer. A healthier world, a happier world, and a more normal world will result from the welcoming of this art than from its suppression. And the world at large is to be congratulated that a recreation has come into vogue which brings the sexes together.

For many years there has been a tendency, especially in America, toward separate pleasures for men and women. Men herded in clubs; women in clubs of their own manless drawing-rooms, where the eternal and brain-dwarfing and body-stiffening bridge game was pursued. Cards are excellent friends to the human race when indulged in occasionally. But nothing is more arresting to mental development, nothing is more unhealthful and unsocial than a card-mania such as the bridge-fobia which has given place now to the dance-ritis.

Women who spent entire days over the bridge-table, beginning in the forenoon and ending at midnight, now meet their men friends at musical dances in the afternoon or balls in the evening. Men who were always in their clubs when not in their offices drop in at musical teas and enjoy dancing at their own homes or the homes of their friends in the evening. On with the dance. It will make the world more wholesome.

XXXV

PRACTICAL MENTAL PRESCRIPTION

I am success. Though hungry, cold, ill-clad,
  I wander for a while; I smile and say,
"It is but for a time—I shall be glad
  To-morrow, for good fortune comes my way.
God is my Father; He has wealth untold,
His wealth is mine, health, happiness, and gold."

On retiring at night, just before going off to sleep, say, either mentally or orally as you choose:

"I am health, strength, peace, happiness, and prosperity, and everything that goes to make for good.

"Pure, good, rich blood is flowing through my body, removing all obstructions and bringing peace, health, and harmony.

"I am well and strong and vital.

"I am beautiful, pure, and good.

"I am on the road to eternal youth.

"I am opulent, happy, and free."

Last, but not least:

"I will arise with unusual energy and radiance and power of accomplishment in the morning."

"All I ask is that you do not try to dictate the way these things shall or may come, and I will guarantee them to cure anything from poverty to rheumatism."—Dr. Carmany.

LET every reader take with seriousness these emphatic statements of Dr. Carmany and put them to the test.

There is nothing the matter with the world, with life, with destiny. Everything we desire or want or need waits for our claiming. But the majority of God's children are waiting for *somebody besides themselves* to bring them these things. Not more than one human being in one thousand looks to *himself* and the Power back of himself for success, health, and happiness. The other nine hundred and ninety-nine look to luck, to chance, to influence, to favors of friends and acquaintances, to doctors, to patent medicines, to some hoped-for miracle, and all the time a mine of wealth and reservoir of power within themselves lies unexplored and unused.

If you have a garden, and a reservoir of water which is fed from an inexhaustible mountain stream, and you spend hours in prayer to God for rain to water your garden, do not feel that God has been unkind if in a season of drought your plants wither and die. It is your own fault that you did not *use the water in the reservoir.*

Prayer is a great force; it puts our highest mental and moral powers in touch with the whole magnificent universe, and with the clouds of witnesses and the hosts of ministering angels who are waiting to do the Father's bidding on earth; and the Father's bidding is eternal usefulness to humanity.

These Invisible Helpers are ever ready to *help us help ourselves.* But they would not answer our prayers for rain to save our gardens if we did not use the water in the reservoir which had been supplied to us. An inexhaustible reservoir lies in every soul born upon earth. The one thing for you to do is to *pipe your mental faculties to this reservoir.*

Then follow the instructions which are quoted above. Every time you make those assertions you are *turning on a faucet.* It is of little use, in a dry, arid season, to turn the water on your garden *once a week.* It must be done *every day.* If you watered your plants once, and then after a month complained how badly they looked despite your having watered them, that would be as reasonable as the attempts of many people to put metaphysical thought into practice. Every trade, profession, business, and art is brought to perfection by *persistent and unremitting efforts.*

The great philosophy of *thought power* can only be proven and demonstrated by the same unremitting, untiring methods. The little formula given by Dr. Carmany holds the whole philosophy in a concise form. It is a spiritual homeopathic tablet. Take one every night on retiring, and after three months you will be astonished at results.

Pray often; lift your heart on high; but *work first, last, and always.* Do not be a spiritual loafer and expect angels to perform your work with no effort on your part. Do not talk about your methods; and do not ask any one for advice or counsel. Look only to your own soul for light.

XXXVI

THE NEED OF THE WORLD

The earth is God's expression,
And love is all it needs;
And this is faith's confession
Of what it lacks in creeds.

THERE is only one need in the world, the need to love our neighbor as ourselves; to do exactly as we would be done by; to understand that the human race is one body, and that when we do anything which harms or hurts one individual we harm all individuals, ourselves included; just as we harm the body when we injure any member—hand, foot, eye, or ear. When we stop and think about the world, the whole process of life becomes very pitiful. Each being born upon the earth is striving for happiness from the cradle to the grave, in his own way.

According to his light, he is doing the best he can. He does not know it, but the only satisfying things which he can get out of life are peace of mind, self-respect, and the love of his fellow-men.

Nothing he can obtain without these things,

nothing he can achieve or become, is of any real value. No man can be happy without these three blessings. Any man can be happy with them, even though he is saddened by the sorrow he sees about him, the sorrow which results from striving after the needless things of earth, after the possessions of others.

There would be no war, no industrial problems, no prisons, no poor-houses, no white slaves, no sex sins if men and women all set forth early in life on that threefold quest—for peace of mind, for self-respect, for the love of their fellow-men.

That is all any soul is seeking; that is all any soul desires, because that is all there is in life worth living for. Yet is there war and strife, hatred and sin, sorrow and anguish, misery and poverty because all men have not yet learned that there is only one need in the world.

The need of the world is *love*. And love is God. Once we love humanity with the love that substitutes pity for censure, we have found God.

The query is put, "How can we love our neighbor as ourself if our neighbor is all that is unlovable, aggressive, disagreeable, immoral, offensive?" This is a conundrum which has vexed many a mind many a time. To encounter people whom it is impossible to love in any degree is a positive pain, since in loving and admiring God's handiwork is the greatest of life's joys.

Fortunately, most people possess some lovable

quality—or at least some admirable trait. The most we can do in our early efforts to live up to the divine injunction is to feel pity or compassion and sympathy for the utterly disagreeable and unlovable beings whom we encounter along life's pathway, instead of allowing dislike and hatred to dominate our minds. If we pause to consider the subject dispassionately we will realize that no sane human being wishes to be disagreeable and unlovable. It is a misfortune brought on by perverted conditions or wrong bringing up and accented by habit. Once we realize this truth we will be sorry for the person we have been inclined to abhor. And pity, we know, is akin to love. The next step in our own self-development is to make an effort to illustrate the benefit and happiness of being agreeable toward our disagreeable neighbor.

This is more easily recommended in print than achieved in conduct. When your "neighbor" entertains you by telling you all the unpleasant gossip or malicious remarks she has heard about you it is difficult to bring yourself into a state of mind to heap coals of fire upon her head by paying her compliments. Yet if you can conscientiously tell her a pleasant thing about herself it is liable to work more of a reformation than any angry sarcasm on your part would do. Just so the "soft answer turneth away wrath" and brings shame to the uncontrolled mind. To show generosity toward the miserly, gentleness toward the violent, charity toward the uncharitable, and unselfishness toward the selfish is an active method of trying to "love our neighbor as ourself."

It is not an easy task. It is much easier to adopt a religion of creeds and forms, to make long prayers in church, to give large sums to charity, to be solemn on Sunday, and from Monday to Saturday to indulge every impulse toward criticism, backbiting, personal grudges, and dislikes; then to repeat, "I believe my sins are redeemed" on the death-bed, and die anticipating a life of glory. This is a popular and pleasant religion.

But it is not the religion of the Golden Rule, nor of the command to "love God with all your heart and your neighbor as yourself."

The former is the religion of our present forms of civilization; the religion of "competition" and "hustling" business methods. The latter is the religion of brotherhood and altruism.

One requires a few hours in the week, the other the continuous effort of a lifetime and a constant watchfulness of self. No great height, geographical, mental, or spiritual, is attained by one sustained attempt. We must climb, fall, and try again and again. The highest possible altitude is that reached by the soul who can truly say, "I love my neighbor, all my neighbors, as myself."

Though we cannot yet say it (and who can?),

we may at least strive to treat our neighbors as we would be treated and to search for the admirable quality in each, forgetting as much as possible the disagreeable traits, even as we would have our own forgotten.

XXXVII

THE LIFE HEREAFTER

Though the ranks of friends are thinning,
Still the end is but beginning
  Of a larger, fuller day;
And the joy of life is spilling,
From my spirit, as all willing
  I go speeding on my way.

A MAN who says he is a great student of all the religions urges me to be "sensible" and discontinue writing or talking about "God" or "Heaven" or "Future Life."

He says these things are superstitions, which people of intellect must abandon or resign all claim to intellectuality.

This man is, of course, an egotist of the rankest order. He is so blinded by his self-conceit that he cannot see Truth. He is like an individual who sits holding his own photograph close to his eyes and says, "There is no universe, no sun or skies; there is only this card on which I see my face." The perfectly balanced human being forms a complete triangle. Physically strong, mentally strong, spiritually strong: the three natures are in perfect harmony.

We find few such beings, and consequently the world is filled with those who are in some respects dwarfed or deformed. There is the robust athlete, whose prowess lies in the physical realm. He has not developed his brain or his spirit. There is the hysterical spiritual being, who thinks only of the world beyond and neglects his mind and his body. There is the intellectual giant who has a stunted body and no spirituality, or who has two sides of the triangle developed, body and mind, and only a blank space where the spiritual line should be.

No one of these individuals is living the life God wants man to live. Each one must be sent back to earth in many incarnations until he learns to make the perfect triangle of himself, and then, being complete, he can pass on to other work in other mansions in other realms.

This man may be a strong man physically and mentally, but he is dwarfed and stunted spiritually; and because he is so he thinks there is no spiritual truth in the universe, as the man born blind might think there was no light of sun or moon or star.

Fortunately, there are hundreds of brilliant minds ready to give their testimony to the contradiction of this man's statement — *viz.*, that earth and human life are accidents, that chance rules all things, and that there is no life beyond this life and no realm beyond earth.

One of the greatest men who ever lived, a

great scientist, a great humanitarian, a great scholar, was Swedenborg. And this man gave up position and power and place among the ambitious people of earth to devote his mature years to telling the world the marvelous facts he had learned about Realms within Realms and Life beyond Life.

When he was dying at the advanced age of eighty-three he was offered all the solaces of orthodox religion if he would say that he had not heard these voices or seen these visions. "But I did see and did hear," he replied. And those were almost his last words.

Swedenborg's opinions on politics or science left no marked impression on the world; very few people even know that he was renowned in those ways. But Swedenborg's religious philosophy is the comfort and the strength of thousands of intellectual and useful human beings.

There is an old Hindu saying which reads thus:

> He who knows not, and knows not that he knows not, he is a fool; shun him.
>
> He who knows not, and knows that he knows not, he is simple; teach him.
>
> He who knows, and knows not that he knows, he is asleep; wake him.
>
> He who knows, and knows that he knows, he is wise; follow him.

Swedenborg was the latter. He was the perfect triangle. Great in all ways. There are thousands of other human beings living, and thousands who have lived, strong of intellect, clear of mind, who have given to the world their testimony of absolute knowledge of the existence of invisible worlds about us, and invisible helpers near us, just as travelers on our earth report different conditions and different scenes in northern and southern and arctic and equatorial locations. So the various seers observe various conditions in the spiritual worlds. There is just as much variety in these realms as in our own, and each seer sees according to his own powers of sight and according to his own mental and spiritual development.

The architect on earth who is absorbed wholly in buildings takes a walk with an artist who cares only for nature, and one returns unable to tell anything about the plants, trees, flowers, or scenery, but everything about the style of houses he has seen; while the artist has not even noticed a house, but is filled with facts concerning the landscape, the streams, the trees, the verdure.

Precisely so with the man who has the open eye in spiritual realms. I know a quiet, industrious business man, respected by his fellows, loved by his associates, who seeks neither glory nor riches and who is ever ready to serve his friends or his enemies with good deeds. This man has the open eye, and he is privileged in being able to see the invisible realms and the invisible helpers who move about among us. Naturally possessed of the clear-seeing eye, he has developed the power of the "initiate" by high thinking and living and preparation. There are a few such on earth, and to meet and talk with them is to gain a great spiritual uplift.

Without a faith in other states of existence, this life at its brightest and best would be insupportable to a finely organized and loving soul. The sudden calamities which befall dear ones, the sorrows and tragedies which come into every life, would make this brief stay on earth a ghastly jest were it not that we know it as only one room in our Father's mansion, and that we are to enter other rooms, dressed in other bodies, after we have passed from this.

Other realms, other lives await us. Earth is but one of many spheres through which we pass. We shall meet and recognize those who were our spiritual kin in these other realms. Vital, deep, beautiful affection can never die. Only ephemeral loves die with death.

Ambition for worldly honors, enjoyment of wholly physical pleasures, and all that is based on selfishness and avarice eventually die with the body. They continue for a time after death because they have fettered the spirit and prevented it from progressing at once. They make the spirit earth-bound for a season, but after a time the spirit gains its knowledge of higher ideals of happiness and goes on to the various heavens, and from those higher heavens it is allowed to come at times to earth to sustain and uplift and help those who remain.

There is no death. There are no dead.

THE END

CPSIA information can be obtained at www.ICGtesting.com
Printed in the USA
BVOW04s0049221214

380413BV00024B/298/P